AMERICAN LAW and the TRAINED FIGHTER

by Carl Brown

Editor: Todd Henschell
Graphic Design: Karen Massad

© 1983 Ohara Publications, Inc.
All rights reserved
Printed in the United States of America
Library of Congress Catalog Number: 83-062220
ISBN: 0-89750-091-1

This book is dedicated to the
lasting memory
of my late Sensei,
Richard "Dick" Falls—
may he rest in peace.

ABOUT THE AUTHOR

Former Jefferson County Commisioner Carl Brown first encountered martial arts while growing up in Louisville's West End. He studied under the late Richard Falls, and earned a black belt in judo. The discipline of martial arts has gained a permanent place in Brown's life. He has carried the judoka's outlook with him to become one of Kentucky's most outstanding citizens. Brown graduated from Vanderbilt University School of Law in Nashville in the top 15 percent of his class, and moved on to a career in law and public service. He has drafted legislation for Kentucky and Tennessee as a member of the Legislative Reference Bureau, worked on the Energy and Environment Task Force, and is a member of the National Association of County Officials. Brown taught at the University of Louisville for three years and also instructed judo classes at the local YMCA. He has authored other books on the relationship of martial arts to the law, and has had an article on the same subject appear in KARATE ILLUSTRATED magazine.

In addition to being politically active, Brown is involved in many social groups. He is the vice-president of the YMCA of Kentucky, serves on the board of directors of the Boy's Clubs of Louisville, and is on the Governmental Affairs Committe of the Metropolitan Louisville United Way. Brown is also the Southeastern United States Representative of the National Society of Youth Governors, and was voted the "Outstanding Young Kentuckian" by the Kentucky Jaycees.

INTRODUCTION

In the ongoing debate of martial arts circles, one argues about the purpose of one's training, and most people admittedly join self-defense schools quite simply to learn how to defend themselves without using weapons. Though thousands of martial artists are interested in the traditions of improving character, physical fitness, and mental well-being, most Americans originally encounter their local *dojo* (gym) as a way to feel more confident about their ability to protect themselves.

This leads us to some questions: Do you have an automatic right to defend yourself in any way you feel necessary? Are you immune to assault and battery charges or civil lawsuits brought against you by someone you injured while defending yourself? If threatened with harm, are you justified in taking *any* action you deem necessary to protect yourself? How about your sweetheart? Your automobile?

All who train in the martial arts today should be aware of some specific court rulings that might bear on their actions. You don't have as many simple, clear-cut rights as you think. Brandishing your martial arts skills may lead to arrest, or a costly and complicated lawsuit.

This is why attorney and judo black belt Carl Brown wrote this book. There are legal ramifications in defending yourself, be it in your home, a neighborhood bar, a parking lot or elsewhere. Different legal constraints may apply to your actions. And remember, the courts always assume you are aware of the legal limits of your actions. The old legal maxim, "Ignorance of the law is no defense," applies here, as well.

American law varies from state to state, and some laws have changed only slightly in a century. Others have changed from year to year, as new circumstances arise. While no book can claim to cover all the issues relating to physical action when defending yourself, *American Law and the Trained Fighter* can help you sort the major issues out.

Carl Brown examines the record of American law concerning assault and battery, explains what legally defines excessive force, what reasonable presumptions apply to self-defense, and what constitutes an "anticipatory attack." (Attacking when you believe *you* will be attacked if you don't act.) Brown also details special areas for the "trained fighter." He tells why a trained fighter may be held accountable because a special standard governing his actions is applied, and he explains the yardstick used in that standard. A court may consider a black belt to be an "expert" in self-defense, so the rules of how well he judged the force of his reaction are stiffer.

Most courts expect an individual to retreat before taking any violent physical action. If you're capable of escaping from an attacker, you should do so before breaching the peace. There's one important exception, and that's when you've been confronted by an intruder in your home. In this case, you have the right *not* to retreat.

The author provides many examples of court cases which illuminate legal trends, and tell you how you can expect to be treated if you overstep your legal boundries. It's important that you know what *could* happen if you do defend yourself violently.

While Carl Brown does give some hypothetical examples, and offers advice based upon legal precedents and his own professional experience, this book can't be considered a cure-all. It will not protect you from a lawsuit or criminal charges, and it *does not* intend to substitute for good legal counsel. It can guide you through the complicated maze of law as it regards self-defense.

If you ever have to defend yourself with force, and doing so lands you in a court battle, you should get an attorney. There's no substitute for a competent lawyer, skilled in the law, experienced in the courtroom. That's an entirely different skill than what's used on the street.

CONTENTS

CHAPTER ONE

The Martial Arts

Chapter One

he United States is exploding with interest in the martial arts. At the outset, it is interesting to note that when we speak of "martial," we refer to something "of, relating to, or suited for war." In contrast, the Japanese word for martial is composed of two components—"stop" and "spear," depicting "martial" in a purely defensive sense.

Specifically, the four arts believed to be most prevalent in America will be explored: karate, jujitsu, judo, and aikido. Naturally, however, the "American arts" of boxing and wrestling, while not singled out for discussion, produce trained fighters just like the Oriental martial arts.

Karate is both a fighting art and a sport. Its name is composed of the Japanese words *kara* (empty) and *te* (hands)—thus, *karate* means to combat weaponless—with "empty hands." History has obscured karate's origins. Some contend its development can be traced to Okinawa, although the basic concept was borrowed from Chinese boxing. Others focus on its relatively late Japanese influence where, disarmed by an Emperor's decree, peasants trained secretly to overcome the armor of the samurai, the warriors and bodyguards of the *daimyo*. The most widely held and authoritative view traces karate's origins to the ingenuity of Indian and Chinese monks who lived with the dilemma of making trade journeys through dangerous, bandit-laden mountains while restricted by their religion from lifting weapons against other human beings. These monks developed their own bodies into potent weapons for self-defense. By pounding their hands and feet on rocks, these monks transformed their natural appendages into deadly club-like weapons. Legend has it that the monks, after disarming and battering their surprised assailants, would bandage and comfort the bandits before resuming their journey. A Buddhist monk named Boddhidharma is most often named as being the founder of this weaponless fighting art, the forerunner of karate.

Karateka (literally, karate practitioners) attack and defend, both in contest and on the street, not only with punches and open-hand blows, but also with knees, elbows, feet, and even the head. Punches and kicks are the most frequently used techniques. The punches are straight, directed along the body's centerline and tend to be thrown with an exaggerated hip movement in order to get full body weight behind the blow. Kicks are slower but more powerful and deceptive. The angle of approach is difficult to predict. For example, a front kick starts with the knee raised to the chest, but from there can assault the groin with a front snap kick, or strike the skull with a roundhouse kick. Many karateka, like their Buddhist monk predecessors, toughen their hands and feet. Typically, a *makiwara* (a large flat board with extra wood and padding attached) is used for this purpose. Methodical kicking and punching of the makiwara toughens the feet and edges of the hands. Upon delivery, karateka utter yells known as *kiai*. This serves the dual purposes of startling the opponent and stimulating the karateka's own adrenalin flow.

These are numerous styles of karate. By country, the Japanese, Chinese and Korean styles command the greatest following among hundreds of thousands of American karate practitioners. To name a few, shotokan, Goju-ryu, Shito-ryu, kenpo, tae kwon do, and kung fu are prominent Oriental "boxing" styles practiced by Americans. The latter two deserve special mention. Though its origins are ultimately traceable to China, as are the other styles, many Koreans take exception to tae kwon do being lumped together with other forms of karate, apparently more for reasons of nationalism than logic. In a similar vein, many kung fu artists resist being labeled "karateka" since kung fu is a general term encompassing many styles of Chinese boxing. Karate and kung fu do share some fundamental hand-and-foot techniques. However, kung fu lays greater stress than karate on finger blows (clawing and stabbing) to the eyes and throat. Whether fact or fiction, some kung fu practitioners of old claim the legendary ability to deliver "death touches." These distinctions not withstanding, for the purposes of this book, "karate" will include any Oriental martial art which teaches hand blows and kicks.

These hand blows and kicks are potent forces. Peasants of feudal Okinawa could subdue armed opponents with their bare hands and feet. It is widely believed that the hands of a karate expert can be as lethal as a hammer. Though vast numbers of Americans have witnessed some karateka break amazing amounts of wood, brick, stone, and ice, few have witnessed the awesome power displayed more dramatically than by men such as Mas Oyama, a major figure in karate's development. Oyama killed a bull with his bare hands, proving karate can be dangerous for bricks, boards, *and* living things.

Jujutsu, more commonly known as jujitsu, unlike karate and judo, has no sport dimension. It is raw self-defense. However, the Japanese term means "art of softness." This seeming inconsistency is resolved in that the jujitsu artist defeats his or her opponent by "appearing to yield." Like karate, there is no small dispute about the origin of jujitsu among historians.

Some claim jujitsu paralleled the development of karate and was originated by Buddhist monks for protection against marauders. More probable, however, is that jujitsu was developed indigenous to Japan and dates back as far as 230 B.C. No less a scholar than Dr. Jigoro Kano, the founder of judo (which is the clear and direct descendant of jujitsu), states conclusively that jujitsu differed so radically from karate that it could not have come from China; rather, it developed in Japan when peasants were forbidden to wear swords. Eventually, the samarai were compelled to learn jujitsu. It became part of their code of honor to attempt to defeat their opponents with jujitsu before drawing their sword.

As indicated, jujitsu is purely for self-defense. Additionally, jujitsu teaches how to throw, choke, lock joints, and hold—these latter four elements forming the basis for judo.

Judo, now part of the Olympic games, is practiced more as a sport than for self-defense, although its utility for self-defense is unquestioned. *Judo* (the gentle way) is "the art of giving way." Knowledgeable historians unanimously concur that judo was derived from jujitsu and systemized in 1882 by Jigoro Kano, an eminent Japanese physical educator and lecturer. Kano refined the harsh jujitsu techniques, purging them of their inherently deadly aspects, and added new techniques of his own. The test of fire came for Kano's new system in 1886. Declining jujitsu schools resented the growing popularity of judo. A national tournament was held under the auspices of the Metropolitan Police Department between 15 of Kano's students and 15 of the best jujitsu practitioners from the outstanding Totsuka School. Kano's *judoka* (judo practitioners) reigned supreme, winning 13 of the matches, drawing two.

Kano put forth two great judo principles: 1) Maximum efficiency with minimum effort, and 2) mutual benefit and welfare. These were the two pillars of the "code of humanitarian ethics" that Kano contributed to the martial arts. This code, and the gentleness of its propagator, is best illustrated by Kano's final match. During a voyage to Europe, Kano, a short, slight man, met a huge Russian in a wrestling match. To the dismay of the spectators, who expected the Russian to easily overpower the small Japanese, Kano threw his opponent effortlessly. "To make this all the more remarkable, he placed his hand under the Russian's head to keep him from hurting it on the floor when he fell.'' Despite the international popularity of Kano and judo, he was poisoned as his ship sailed between America and Japan, and the circumstances of his death are still mysterious. Today, Kano's picture hangs in every judo dojo, and all students bow to his image before and after each class as a show of respect.

Although it's difficult to determine precisely the number of judoka in America, judo commands an impressive following. As both an Olympic and as an AAU (American Athletic Union) sport, its ranks have increased impressively. Some estimate judo has between 40,000 and 50,000 active practitioners. Judo appeals to the young and old—Kyuzo Mifune, a great moving influence in judo, practiced actively until his death at age 81; and to persons in all walks of life—Theodore Roosevelt worked out regularly at the White House under a protege of Kano, and gained exceptional skill.

Judo's characterization as ''gentle'' is deceptive. It is very rough and effective. However, the muscular strength so vital to boxing and wrestling is less important in judo. In fact, the weight and strength of *your opponent* provide all that is needed for his or her defeat since you use the opponent's weight against himself. This opening gambit of non-resistance contains a built-in element of surprise, since no attacker expects an opponent to fight back by yielding. Judo instructors teach throws, pins, chokes, and armlocks. Judo is unique in that judoka may proceed with wild abandon in practice since judoka are taught how to fall without injury and how to submit when a choke, hold, or armlock becomes dangerous. In contest judo, a premium is placed on coordination between bodily movement and mental strategy, making judo like a game of chess. No better synopsis of judo is available than that given by Jigoro Kano himself in a speech before a University of Southern California audience, on the occasion of the Tenth Olympiad, 1932:

Let me now explain what this gentleness or giving way really means. Suppose we assume that we may estimate the strength of man in units of one. Let us say that the strength of man standing in front of me is represented by ten units, whereas my strength, less than his, is represented by seven units. Then if he pushes me with all his force I shall certainly be pushed back or thrown down, even if I use all my strength against him. This would happen because I used all my strength against him, opposing strength with strength. But if, instead of opposing him, I were to give way to strength by withdrawing my body just as much as he had pushed remembering to keep my balance, then he would naturally lean forward and thus lose his balance. In this new position, he may have become weak (not in actual physical strength but because of his awkward position) as to have his strength represented for the moment by, say, only three units, instead of his normal ten units. But meanwhile, I, by keeping my balance, retain my full strength, as originally represented by seven units. Here then, I am momentarily in an advantageous position and I can defeat my opponent using only half of my strength, that is half of my seven units, or three and one-half of my strength against his three. This leaves one-half (units) of my strength available for any purpose. In case I had greater strength than my opponent I could of course push him back. But even in this case, that is, if I had wished to push him back and had the power to do so, it would be better first for me to have given way, because in doing so I should have greatly economized my energy.

Aikido is the most mystical martial art. Founded in 1925 by Japan's Morihei Uyeshiba, it is the most modern of Japan's fighting arts. Aikido means "accumulated force," the unity of thought and action. It is a fluid, circular, potent martial art that is based on the thought that all bodily movements agree with the laws of nature. Aikido teaches throws, wrist and armlocks, and escapes, applied in circular rather than linear movements. Since there are few aikido schools in America and since it takes long years to become moderately proficient, one high estimate of its American practitioners is a mere 6,000.

Clearly, boxing, wrestling, *sumo,* etc., qualify as much as fighting arts as the Japanese arts discussed. However, for the purpose of discussion, this book will concentrate on the Oriental arts of self-defense (and offense). Nevertheless, it is important to stress that *trained fighters* are the focus of this book, regardless of the specific art or arts in which one becomes proficient.

CHAPTER TWO

Assault and Battery

Of all the topics in this book, this one is the most difficult to discuss. A trained fighter should be the last one to ever use his or her skills in an aggressive, unprovoked manner. Happily, such instances are rare in the martial arts world—no doubt due to the discipline instilled in martial artists by the ethics of the Oriental arts (and the calm that comes from attaining black belt or "expert" status). But whether or not you are the actual cause of a physical incident, you may still be accused of assault and battery.

Assault and battery is two-faceted: the civil offense and the criminal offense. Further, while usually mentioned in the same breath, you should understand that assault and battery are separate offenses. Simply put, *assault* is acting in such a way as to put another in *imminent apprehension* of physical harm. *Battery* is carrying through with hitting, kicking, gouging or otherwise *harmful contact* with the person. It requires physical contact between the parties.

Criminal assault and battery brings a new issue to bear—namely, whether your hands and feet can be considered deadly weapons. American courts are split on this subject. Numerous defendants have been charged with *aggravated* assault (an offense with greater consequences than simple assault) for injuring others with their bare hands or feet. This contrasts with the norm, where aggravated assault usually refers to assaults with inanimate objects such as pipes or knives.

Courts disagree on whether an assault with bare hands can be considered aggravated assault. Some courts have rejected labeling bare hands as dangerous or deadly weapons. The New York Appeals Court, for example, reversed a first-degree manslaughter conviction, holding "when the legislature talks of a 'dangerous weapon,' it means something quite different from the bare fist of an *ordinary* man" (author's emphasis). In a similar case, *State* v. *Calvin,* the Louisiana Supreme Court conceded that bare hands are capable of producing "death or great bodily harm" but nevertheless held that "there must be proof of the use of some inanimate object before a defendant can be held guilty of assault 'with a dangerous weapon.' " Many other courts have ruled that mere use of the hands does not constitute aggravated assault. Other courts, however, have been less definite and have held that bare hands may under certain circumstances be considered "dangerous weapons." So the manner in which your hands and feet are used may be a determining factor.

Most cases where one is charged with aggravated assault with bare hands usually deal with assault with both the hands *and* feet. Without considering the added factor of footwear (shoes, boots, spike heels, etc.), there are several cases that have held that an assault with hands and feet is not assault with a deadly weapon. The landmark case, *Wilson* v. *State,* was decided by the Arkansas Supreme Court in 1924. The defendant had beaten and kicked a physician "in the face and side."

At his trial the defendant was convicted of assault with a deadly weapon. The Arkansas Supreme Court later modified the charge to simple assault and battery because the defendant used *only* hands and feet—therefore, "no deadly weapon was used."

With language that many courts have since adopted, the Arkansas Supreme Court argued that capacity to kill is not the same thing as "assault with a deadly weapon," even though the defendant has unusual ability to fight with his hands and feet:

> *A powerful man—a Dempsey or Firpo—might kill one by striking with the fist or kicking with the foot, but a great bodily injury by these means would not be an assault with a deadly weapon, instrument, or other thing, in the sense of the aggravated assault statute.*

Some commentators have criticized restricting the "deadly/dangerous" weapon label to inanimate objects. Instead of looking to the *object employed,* it has been urged that courts should instead take into account the *potential danger of the method used.* This means that the "deadly/dangerous" weapon test should include, not just guns or knives, but teeth, fists, a guard dog, or any other animate or inanimate object. For example, if only an inanimate object can be dangerous, then the defendant who pokes out the victim's eye with a finger pays the penalty for simple battery while the co-defendant who puts out the victim's other eye with a pencil pays the penalty for an aggravated battery.

Other courts, by contrast, have considered the surrounding circumstances and manner in which the instrument was employed. There are several notable prosecutions where the defendant's hands and/or feet committed the criminal attack. Where hands or fists have been used to inflict death or injury, some courts have held defendants liable under aggravated assault and homicide statutes.

One of the most important cases is *Commonwealth* v. *Buzard,* decided by the Pennsylvania Supreme Court in 1950. The court affirmed the defendant's conviction of second-degree murder where the defendant and the victim argued over a $31 lumber bill. This led to a brawl, and the defendant killed the man by straddling him and beating him with blows to the head with his fists. The defendant was taller than the victim by a full six inches and outweighed him by more than 40 pounds. In upholding the defendant's conviction, the Pennsylvania Supreme Court observed:

> *Fists, though not ordinarily a deadly weapon, may become deadly by repeated and continued blows applied to vital and delicate parts of the body of the defenseless, unresisting victim.*

The Pennsylvania Supreme Court thus isolated two elements which could turn fists into deadly weapons: "repeated and continued blows" and administration of these blows to "vital and delicate parts of the body" (a third, lesser element could be found in a "defenseless, unresisting victim"). In *Quarles* v. *State,* the Georgia Appeals Court held that the jury could consider fists to be deadly weapons, "depending on the manner and means of their use, the wounds inflicted, etc." The court refused to hold as a matter of law that fists were *not* deadly weapons. In *People* v. *Score,* the California Appeals Court expanded this concept of "special use" while upholding a conviction of assault by means or force likely to produce great bodily harm. The court noted that a proper list of elements for jury consideration would include "the force of the impact, the manner in which (the fist) was used and the circumstances under which the force was applied."

These examples reveal the analytical approach courts take when determining if the defendant's hands were used to produce a second-degree murder or aggravated assault. Apart from the question of footwear (inanimate weapon), courts view the use of feet similarly to the way they view the use of hands in producing a criminal assault. In *State* v. *Johnson,* decided by the Missouri Supreme Court in 1927, the drunken defendant was found smacking and "kinda stamping" on his wife as he sat on the edge of a boat and she lay in muddy water. The court held that, while the state proved defendant's guilt of common assault, it had failed to prove defendant's guilt of assault with felonious intent. However, the court also observed that a felonious assault "could be committed by a strong man *viciously kicking* another in the *head or in some vital part of the body* with feet encased in heavy shoes or boots" (author's emphasis).

The third setting is the most common, where the defendant used both hands and feet in assaulting the victim. When hands and feet combine to assault a victim, it is generally held they may become deadly weapons "when used in such manner and in such circumstances as are reasonably calculated to produce death." Four cases shed light on these "manner and circumstances." First, *Lyon* v. *Commonwealth* brought to the attention of the Kentucky Court of Appeals a case where the defendant beat and kicked his elderly (over 65), 135-pound father-in-law for insulting him and shaking a fist in the defendant's face. After examining indictments in cases of this nature, the court instructed that:

> *If the instrument alleged to have been used is less formidable and deadly than the ordinary things with which homicide is generally produced, then the indictment should aver that the said intrumentality used by the defendant was a deadly weapon when employed by him in a way and manner set forth in the indictment.*

Some 26 years later the Kentucky Court of Appeals, hearing *Vogg* v. *Commonwealth,* cited that ruling to show the judicial inconsistency in this area of the law. The court affirmed the defendant's conviction for "assault with deadly weapon with intent to kill"—the defendant prisoner had grabbed the jailer "like they teach in the army" (where the defendant formerly had served as a paratrooper), threw the jailer to the ground, then beat and kicked him. The jailer was so badly injured that his doctor "for two hours or more . . . believed the man had died." Confronted with the facts, the Kentucky Court of Appeals, apparently ignoring Kentucky precedent to the contrary, held "hands and feet . . . are to be regarded as within the term 'deadly weapon' only when used in such manner and in such circumstances as are reasonably calculated to produce death."

To these elements of "manner" and "circumstances reasonably calculated to produce death," the Minnesota Supreme Court in its 1968 *State* v. *Born* decision added the express consideration (implicit in the *Vogg* opinion) of *extent of injuries.* In this controversy, the defendant approached his victim in a laundry, shook and pushed him, pursued him, and knocked him down, then brutally kicked him as he lay on the floor "without effective means of defense." The court was faced with the question of whether such an attack was an assault covered under Minnesota Statutes, making criminal "assault with a dangerous weapon but without intent to inflict great bodily harm." To support the inference not only that the defendant wore shoes, but also that the defendant "used his feet and fists in such a way as to make these appendages dangerous weapons," the court looked among other things, to "the nature of the injuries sustained by the victim." In accord is *State* v. *Golladay,* discussed in detail later, where the murder victim's bodily injuries provided the vehicle through which the state introduced evidence of the defendant's training in karate and jujitsu.

To complete this analysis, *Pulliam* v. *State,* decided by the Mississippi Supreme Court in 1974, contributes the element of *force* to the list of elements court use to decide whether hands and feet are deadly/dangerous weapons. Following an accident, the defendant dragged the victim from his truck, and (according to the victim) knocked him to the ground, then started kicking him in the face and chest. The victim suffered two broken ribs and multiple face laceration. The court reversed and sent back the defendant's conviction, noting that it was a reversible error for the trial judge to instruct the jury that hands and feet are deadly weapons. The Mississippi Supreme Court remarked: "While the use of feet and fists ordinarily would not constitute the use of a deadly weapon, they can constitute a deadly weapon if used with *means or force likely to produce death*" (author's emphasis).

"Special Use" of Hands and Feet

In each of the discussed factual situations, defendant's use of hands, defendant's use of feet, and defendant's use of hands and feet, the courts—consciously or not—dealt with issues of "special use." This justified prosecuting the various defendants under aggravated assault (and homicide) statutes since the nature or extent of the assaults were extreme. In the majority of cases, the "special use of hands and feet" meant the assault was vicious or callous. "Special," however, implies something else too: trained, skilled, and experienced use of the hands and feet as assault weapons. It is this dimension of "special" that this book addresses.

Courts look to the "special" use of the hands and feet of skilled fighters when deciding whether their hands or feet are deadly weapons within the meaning of aggravated assault statutes. No doubt the Kentucky Court of Appeals was influenced to disregard prior case law by the *Vogg* defendant's use of fighting skills to down the jailer. Likewise, the Iowa Supreme Court in *State* v. *Broten* upheld as relevant the prosecutor's line of questioning that brought out the defendant's record as a Golden Glove boxer. The victim made the fatal mistake of propositioning the defendant's wife. The defendant immediately confronted the victim outside the restaurant. Thereupon, according to the defendant, the victim pushed him. The defendant countered with a left hook that sent the victim crashing to the sidewalk, where he struck his head and died. The Iowa court affirmed the conviction of manslaughter.

In *State* v. *Golladay,* the Washington Supreme Court reviewed the defendant's first-degree murder conviction. Evidence of the defendant's training in karate and jujitsu was shown at the trial. The murder victim's body was marred with heavy bruises on the hands (presumedly caused by defensive actions), along with other facial, thigh, and breast wounds. Certain wounds to the head caused extensive hemorrhaging, resulting in the victim's death. According to the pathologist, "the blows were made with a blunt instrument having a rounded surface." Though the court reversed the conviction on other grounds, it nevertheless held that it was not an error to admit evidence of the defendant's special training in the martial arts:

> *The defendant next urges that the trial court erred in permitting evidence of defendant's training in karate or jujitsu. It is argued that this evidence could only serve to inflame the minds of the jury. This evidence, however, dealt with the physical ability of defendant to inflict the extensive wounds suffered by the victim, some of which being described as defense wounds. The slight prejudice which may have resulted from this evidence did not outweigh its relevancy. There was no abuse of discretion in this matter.*

Aggravated Assaults

The following sections deal with the three ways in which statutes refer to aggravated assaults: assault with a deadly weapon, assault with a dangerous weapon, and assault by means or force likely to cause great bodily injury. The first two sections discuss the shoe as a deadly or dangerous weapon. The third section addresses hands *and* feet as instruments capable of inflicting great bodily injury.

If the defendant employed a deadly weapon, the assault is considered "aggravated." "Deadly weapon" has been variously defined. In *Acres* v. *United States,* the U.S. Supreme Court defined it as "a thing with which death can be easily and readily produced." Also, the deadliness of a weapon will be found where "great or serious injury is likely to result." This raises an inquiry of how shoes might be characterized as deadly weapons. This goes to statutory construction; where courts strictly construe the phrase "deadly weapons." Shoes don't fall within the scope of the statute.

There exists a split regarding whether a shoe can ever constitute a deadly weapon as defined by aggravated assault statutes. The majority view holds that under certain circumstances, it can. Still, some courts strictly construe aggravated assault statutes and hold that ordinary shoes are not deadly weapons. In *Dickson* v. *State,* the Arkansas Supreme Court affirmed the aggravated assault conviction of a defendant who had beaten and kicked the mayor, causing brain damage and a ruptured eardrum. Although testimony established no more than that the mayor was struck with the defendant's hands and shoed feet, the court nevertheless sustained the jury's finding that a deadly weapon was used. Testimony established that the defendant had a pistol at some point before the assault and had time to dispose of it after the assault. The court apparently preferred to infer a pistol-whipping rather than wrestle with the legal questions raised by a finding that the injuries resulted from kicks. This inference was necessary to affirm the conviction since the court noted, "the shoes which a person wears as a part of his ordinary apparel are not deadly weapons, within the meaning of the statute relative to aggravated assault."

The majority of courts hold that shoes *can* be deadly weapons as defined by aggravated assault statutes. Numerous factors are considered. Since the "deadly character" is a by-product of "the manner and circumstances" in which the shoes are used, the question becomes one of fact for the jury. And since shoes are not inherently deadly, the question for the jury to decide is whether a shoe "assumes the characteristics of a deadly weapon." The Colorado Supreme Court in *Grass* v. *People* considered the following elements significant in deciding whether a shoe is a deadly weapon: "The nature of the instrument or thing, the manner of its use, the location on the body of the injuries inflicted and the extent of such injuries."

In *Bass* v. *State,* the Florida court elaborated on "the nature of the instrument or thing." There, the defendant appealed his conviction of assault with a deadly weapon on the grounds that since the assault was with fists and feet only, it could not constitute assault with a deadly weapon within the meaning of the applicable statute. The court distinguished between fists and feet (shoed), noting there might be some merit to the defendant's argument regarding fists "but the same cannot be said for the contention that shoes do not constitute a deadly weapon." The court laid great stress on the particular characteristics of the shoes worn by the defendant at the time of the assault. In an oft-quoted passage, the court observed:

> *Shoes come in all shapes, sizes, forms and materials—from the delicate creations of silk and leather, or satin and plastic, to the cleated, hobnailed, iron-toed, leather-heeled boots of the cowboy—any one of which may be capable of inflicting grievous bodily harm or death. The records of medical science are replete with case histories of persons being seriously wounded or killed after being struck by the high heel of a woman's shoe, or having the "boot put to him" by a strong man. It is a jury question as to whether or not a shoe or boot constitutes a deadly weapon, under all the circumstances surrounding the shoe or boot, its size, weight and construction, and the manner in which it was used.*

Philosophy of the Courts

The extremes to which courts may go in this philosophy is seen in *Johnson* v. *State,* a 1971 Florida decision. The court conceded that a shoe could be a deadly weapon but reversed the defendant's "aggravated assault with a deadly weapon" conviction since "there was no evidence whatsoever that a shoe was involved."

A second aggravated assault is assault with a *dangerous* weapon. Differentiation between a "deadly" weapon and a "dangerous" weapon is more semantic than real. In some cases, it represents a casual word choice more than a policy of gradating offenses. However, since in the minds of some courts, the deadly/dangerous dichotomy represents a difference in degree, separate treatment is justified.

As with "deadly weapons," the concept of "dangerous weapon" entails the capacity to inflict serious injuries. As the District Court for Delaware noted in *United States* v. *Barber* with respect to shoes " . . . almost any object 'which as used or attempted to be used may endanger life or inflict great bodily harm' or (that) which 'is likely to produce death or great bodily injury' can in certain circumstances be a dangerous weapon."

In determining whether a dangerous weapon was used, courts look both to the use and to the nature of the defendant's footgear. Regarding use, *Smith* v. *State,* decided by the Oklahoma Criminal Court of Appeals, lends guidance. There the court heard an appeal from a conviction for assault with a dangerous weapon. The defendant had been prosecuted for hitting and kicking (with heavy shoes) an elderly woman. Since the court found no evidence that *kicking* caused the injury, the conviction was affirmed only as assault and battery. However, the court observed that shoes are not dangerous weapons per se, but can become such "by their manner of use . . . under certain circumstances." The Iowa Supreme Court in *State* v. *Bradley,* the District Court for Delaware in *United States* v. *Barber* and the D.C. Circuit in *Medlin* v. *United States* are in accord.

Regarding the nature of the footgear, the majority and dissenting opinions in *Ransom* v. *State* provide an excellent discussion. In essence, the Alaska Supreme Court overturned the defendant's conviction because the state proved merely that the victim was assaulted with "footgear," not with "boots." The majority used the following analysis to reach its conclusion that the conviction must be overturned:

(We cannot) conclude that the variance between "boots"

and "footgear" is immaterial. It is true that many kinds of shoes could be considered the rough equivalent of boots. However, . . . one of the questions the jury was to answer was whether the "boots" of Ransom were dangerous weapons. Because of this required determination, the physical characteristics of Ransom's footgear cannot be considered immaterial. The term footgear could include such a variety of shoes, sandals, slippers and mukluks besides boots that we cannot see how a jury could reasonably decide whether Ransom's "footgear" was a dangerous weapon.

Concurring in part and dissenting in part, the judge raised a fresh consideration. His contention was that the use of the footgear as "instruments of offensive combat," not whether the footgear was boots or shoes, should largely determine whether an assault with footgear was an assault with a deadly weapon.

Consideration of cases dealing with striking or kicking as assault, by means or force likely to cause great bodily harm, concludes the aggravated assault offense discussion. Such differs from the others in two respects. First, the emphasis shifts from instrumentalities to manner. (This is explicit in the statement of the offense and does not depend on judicial construction for its existence.) Second, *both* hands and feet will be discussed as means of inflicting great bodily harm.

The felonious assault created when one hits or kicks with force, or means likely to cause great bodily harm, need not be carried out with a deadly weapon to fall within the scope of this statutory aggravated assault. It seems clear that the amount of force, not whether an object is used, is the relevant inquiry. For the offense to exist, it is not necessary, quoting the colorful language of a California opinion, "that the victim be held over a blazing furnace or be fired upon with an atomic weapon;" a hit or kick may suffice. The nature and extent of the victim's injuries are relevant and may help determine whether the force was of a felonious character.

Kicking a person in the face and head, for example, has been found to enter the scope of an aggravated assault. Unfortunately, some courts still look to the character of the shoes, even when the prosecution is for assault by means or force likely to cause great bodily harm.

Fists also enter the scope of aggravated assault. They may be used as "a force likely to produce death or great bodily harm." This is true whether or not a deadly weapon is involved. In at least one case, *People* v. *Zankich,* the defendant's closed fist was shown to the jury so they could determine whether it seemed capable of inflicting serious bodily injury. The relevant inquiry is the degree of force utilized by the defendant. In *People* v. *Fuentes,* the California Appeals Court held that a knockout punch to the jaw was not a blow sufficiently powerful to be viewed as a blow likely to cause great bodily injury. That view has subsequently met with disapproval.

The Martial Artists

Before going on to "lessons for the trained fighter," some discussion of the fighting arts and the special ability trained fighters enjoy is needed.

Martial artists, of course, have special fighting abilities—their entire bodies have been transformed into veritable fighting machines. They manifest their abilities in varying ways. Karateka and kung fu practitioners strike with the hands and kick with the feet. Judo, aikido and jujitsu practitioners stress throwing, choking, holding, and arm-locking techniques. Judo and jujitsu also contain striking techniques *(atemi-waza).* For present purposes, emphasis will be given to the striking and kicking techniques of martial artists.

The hands and feet of trained martial artists are flesh-and-blood weapons which can easily inflict injuries comparable to those inflicted by a club or knife. In fact, persons have died at the hand (and feet) of martial artists. For analytical purposes, an examination of this "capacity for destruction" enjoyed by martial artists will focus on three elements, deliberate toughening of the hands and feet, skilled or special use of the hands and feet, and conscious "targeting" of strikes and kicks. To envision these three elements operating in unison, the reader should envision a karateka hurling a hard, toughened fist at some pressure point on the opponent's body. In practice, it is uncommon for any one martial art to lay equal emphasis on all three elements. For example, while judoka do not condition their hands, martial artists in certain styles of karate stress toughening the hands and feet. Jujitsu and kung fu exalt *targeted* blows over *powerful* blows. All striking techniques, however, share the element of "skilled or special use." Each of the mentioned martial arts teaches the proper way to kick or strike in order to maximize the damage inflicted.

The first element is conditioning of the hand or foot—hardening the skin which takes the impact. This prevails in kung fu and certain karate styles. Toughening the hand traditionally has been achieved on a makiwara board. Martial artists repeatedly strike the board with the knuckles and sides of their hands, creating calluses. Additionally, some karateka harden their hands and fingers by sifting them through boxes filled with sand, then rice, then gravel. Kung fu masters allegedly toughen their hands by soaking them in vats of herb juices.

One karateka's routine: Twice a day he struck his dojo's concrete walls 300 times "with enough power to knock out most men;" and concluding the ritual he cut deep grooves into the sides of his hand and first two knuckles of each hand (points of contact for chops and blows) with razor blades and plunged the blood-spurting hand into a white mud mixture made of salt and water.

To condition his hands, Mas Oyama, one of modern karate's fathers, would go to the mountains each winter and camp beside a healthy pine tree. Every morning he would pound the tree 200 consecutive times. When the tree died, Oyama took it as a sign to break camp and leave the mountains.

Bare feet are conditioned in much of the same way described. Karateka Ronnie Barkoot conditioned his feet by running, barefooted, to the top of Atlanta's steep and craggy Stone Mountain, then back down again. When the bare soles hit the sharp rocks, the weight and pressure would pop the skin open, much like a dart hitting a water ballon. Nerves and muscles hung on the bottom, and some of the toes resembled bloody-red cauliflowers.

A second component of the martial artist's personal "capacity for destruction" is the force and manner with which blows and kicks are administered. The manner fuels the force. By *snapping* punches and kicks, returning the fist or foot to its point of departure, the velocity—and therefore power—of the blow or kick is multiplied. This swift recoil not only increases the power, but also removes the foot or fist from the opponent's clutches.

Kicks are more powerful than hand blows. However, strikes with the hand of a skilled martial artist can also be devastating. In killing a healthy bull with his bare hands, Mas Oyama undoubtedly gave the single-most spectacular and decisive display of punching power in martial arts history. Before motion picture cameras, Oyama provoked the bull with well-aimed pebbles, then ran, prompting the beast to give pursuit. Moments before the bull made contact, Oyama twirled and lobbed off a horn with his bare hand. He then battered the bull with deadly blows until it fell to the ground in a lifeless heap. The butcher who carted the dead creature away later claimed that the blows rendered the bull unfit for human consumption.

Martial artists are not limited to striking with the hands and feet. Some break 300-pound blocks of ice with their heads. Similar feats have been performed with elbows and knees.

The third component of this fighting style is the deliberate targeting of kicks and blows. Most prevalent in jujitsu and kung fu, this "targeting" is likewise relevant to non-striking, non-kicking techniques. For example, judo and jujitsu experts apply chokes and armlocks to specific parts of the body to maximize strangulation and joint impairment. Judo and aikido adepts throw opponents by avoiding their opponents, then heaving.

As one college judo instructor pointed out, "Bullies don't have the mentality to learn (judo) because they don't have the patience; they want something quick and easy, and it takes two to three years to do good judo." Some martial arts instructors refuse to teach students who show signs of misusing their knowledge.

Nevertheless, martial artists have committed aggravated assaults. In Pittsburgh, a police officer was injured by a karate-trained suspect. Recently, a mother was sentenced to prison for complicity in the death by beating of her two-year-old daughter —the mother made no attempt to stop her boyfriend and children from practicing karate blows on the two-year-old child.

In determining whether the hands and feet of martial artists are aggravated assault weapons, it is useful to refer again to a 1968 survey. Twenty-six law enforcement agencies were queried whether the use of karate would constitute an aggravated crime, such as assault with a deadly weapon. Nine responses were categorical affirmatives. Eleven other responses indicated that an "assault with a deadly weapon" prosecution *could* be successful, depending on the circumstances.

Under certain circumstances, criminal assaults by unarmed martial artists *should* be treated as aggravated assaults. Quite simply, the hands and feet of martial artists *can* be dangerous weapons, and cause great bodily harm. Implicit in many opinions holding hands and feet not to be deadly or dangerous weapons, is the *Vollmer* court notion (i.e., aggravated assault legislation envisions the "ordinary man" as its potential defendant). Given this assumption, it is reasonable to require the presence of inanimate weapons before prosecuting this ordinary man for aggravated assault. One who by virtue of special training can employ his or her hands and feet as deadly weapons, graduates from "ordinary man" status and should be treated no differently from the knife or club wielder. It is the *result,* serious harm to the victim, or its potential (not whether an animate of inanimate object inflicted that harm), which underpins and justifies aggravated assault statutes. Therefore, it seems that the Arkansas Supreme Court was mistaken when it remarked in its *Wilson* opinion that a blow from Jack Dempsey would not be an assault with a deadly weapon. A blow from Dempsey, or a side-thrust kick from a skilled karateka, should be considered as no less deadly or dangerous than an inept club assault from some hoodlum.

In deciding whether the hands and feet of martial artists were, in fact, employed as aggravated assault weapons, several facts should be determined. Five of the considerations or elements find support in current case law:

— The nature of the injuries received by the victim.
— The force used by the defendant.
— Whether repeated blows were struck.
— The manner or style of attack.
— Whether the blows and kicks were administered to vital areas of the victims's body.

When the defendant is a martial artist, at least two more inquiries should be raised. First, it should be determined whether the defendant has had special training as a fighter and the extent of such training. The importance of this inquiry has been implicitly or explicitly recognized in the *Golladay, Vogg, Broten,* and *Bean* opinions where the criminal defendants were respectively, a karateka, ex-paratrooper, and two boxers. The defendant's skill as a martial artist is important in determining if the assault was deadly, dangerous, or likely to cause great injury. After all, disproportionate power is the ultimate danger against which aggravated assault statutes are designed to protect, not just dangers of attack by use of inanimate weapons.

Two considerations qualify this inquiry into special skill. First, courts should distinguish among martial artists. All other things being equal, the martial arts *expert* could and should more readily be found guilty of aggravated assault (than the *novice* martial artist). It is only the expert who can wield hands and feet as dangerous or deadly weapons. In measuring expertise, courts will find belt ranks a convenient yardstick. The professionally taught expert should be distinguished from the self-taught/paperback-taught "expert." Those falling in this category possess no true or unique skill and should be treated the same as non-martial artists.

A second inquiry should be made about the condition of the martial artist's hands and feet. As discussed earlier, many martial artists deliberately harden their hands and feet into club-like weapons. Many of the same considerations courts have given to the weight, size, texture, etc., of a shoe logically could apply to the *bare* hands or *bare* feet of a martial artist. Authority already exists for showing the defendant's fist to the jury, like an exhibit, for purposes of illustrating its weapon-like character.

When martial artists are prosecuted for aggravated assault, the presence or absence of shoes loses relevance. While it may be true that shoes enhance the ability of laypersons to inflict injury, the opposite is often true for martial artists. Martial artists train barefooted, kicking with the ball, heel, and side of the foot. Kicks are faster and more accurately targeted when delivered shoeless. Moreover, kicks to the face and flying kicks are easier to execute when barefooted. These bare feet of karateka are often more dangerous than the booted feet of laypersons. Therefore, the *Johnson* extreme, where the state's failure to prove the defendant wore shoes resulted in a reversal of the defendant's conviction for assault with a deadly weapon, isn't logical if applied to martial artists. There are martial artists whose first impulse in street encounters is to kick off shoes in order to improve their kicking techniques. The Alaska Supreme Court justice was on the right track when he argued that the *kind of footgear* employed was a secondary consideration compared with the matter of whether the feet were used as "instruments of offensive combat."

The danger is that martial artists will be perfunctorily prosecuted for aggravated assaults when the evidence might call for a simple assault prosecution. Martial artists can "pull" punches and kicks, lessening their impact. They can use non-deadly techniques. And they can simply use non-martial arts modes of fighting. Therefore, while martial artists are deadly fighters, it would be unfair to assume that their hands and feet were used as deadly or dangerous weapons, unless the evidence supports such a finding.

Apart from judicial determination that hands or feet were used as deadly weapons, attention must be given to regulatory legislation. There exists a popular American belief that martial artists must register their hands as deadly weapons with the police department. Whatever the source of this "modern myth," its survival and propagation has been aided by uninformed martial artists as well as uninformed laypersons. A 1968 survey categorically and unequivocally denied that karateka had to "register their hands as deadly weapon." This, of course, begs the real question—is such registration desirable?

While it is true that few, if any, legal restrictions are uniquely imposed on martial artists, this writer nevertheless feels "registration" affords no solution. In the first place, the enforcement problem would be staggering. Should law enforcement officers be successful in securing registration of the untold thousands of martial artists who have received professional instruction, this leaves unregistered an invisible mass of "martial artists" who have had no formal instruction. While these paperback-martial artists are less dangerous, they are far more likely to become criminal defendants. A second problem exists in the logical inconsistency posed by registering martial artists. Pocketknife wielders have similar abilities to harm others (though perhaps to a lesser degree). Pocketknife wielders, in fact, may pose a greater social danger than martial artists since martial artists are prone to avoid all street encounters by virtue of their training. Third, and last, no vital state interest would be served by registration of martial artists. This can be contrasted with registering firearms. Registration of firearms makes sense because lost or stolen firearms can be used by others to commit crimes. Firearm registration provides names, leading to suspects. Registration of martial artists would serve no similar purposes. The hands and feet of martial artists cannot be used by others. Severe injuries can be inflicted by large, untrained men, or small men with bludgeons. Registration isn't a cure-all.

CHAPTER THREE

Self-Defense and the Trained Fighter

elf-defense is not simply a right, but according to the law, it's also a "privilege." That means if the legal limits of action is exceeded, it can be lost. The martial artist, then, should understand how *not* to exceed, therefore lose, this self-defense privilege. In fact, self-defense raises a number of distinct issues for martial artists, namely:

— Was the martial artist in fear of apprehension?
— Was there a duty to retreat?
— Was the force used excessive, or reasonable?
— Was the martial artist able to measure with precision the force used?
— Was there a right to "anticipatorily attack" (pre-emptive strike)?

For the average trained fighter, this section on self-defense will be the heart of the book. Martial artists, for example, have responded (and over-responded) to attacks and have wound up being sued or criminally prosecuted. If the reader is aware of the laws explained here, the chances of that happening should be reduced.

Both civil and criminal law contain the privilege of self-defense. Subtle distinctions can be drawn, but that would just complicate the analysis—especially since self-defense occurs in the heat of the moment and "subtle distinctions" would be lost in the fray anyway.

The privilege of self-defense is triggered only where the "actor" is apprehensive about being assaulted. These fears must be reasonable. In assessing the fear, one authority suggests that the "difference in age, size, and relative strength of the parties" would be helpful. The actor must be apprehensive about serious bodily harm or death to justify self-defense with killing force. However, the actor need not fear for his life or safety to justify a *lesser* degree of force in self-defense.

It is clear that a defendant's failure to actually *fear* his opponent will not affect the defendant's right to self-defense. Apprehension is not the same thing as fear. For example:

> *Mr. A, a scrawny individual who is intoxicated, attempts to strike Mr. B with his fist, who is the heavyweight boxing champion of the world. B is not at all afraid of A, is confident he can avoid any such blow, and in fact succeeds in doing so. A is subject to liability to B.*

Apprehension gives rise to the privilege of self-defense, since one is permitted by law to fend off an assault. One need not fear the intended contact will be successful; one need only believe the act may result in imminent contact unless prevented by flight or intervention.

The person about to defend himself or herself may be under a duty to warn his or her assailant of such intention. Apparently this is true only when there is reason to believe a warning will deter the attack, and also allow the person time to defend himself or herself, if still necessary. This issue is related to "apprehension" in that it pertains to the defendant's state of mind at the time of self-defense.

North Dakota, Oklahoma and Louisiana courts have

spoken on the nature of the fear or apprehension necessary to warrant self-defense in civil cases. In 1926, the North Dakota Supreme Court heard *Powell* v. *Meiers.* There, the defendant and another called on the plaintiff's home to borrow a gun. Refusing the request, the plaintiff chided the defendant for taking money from her son in poker games. The defendant retorted by calling the plaintiff "ugly names" and by casting "grave imputations upon her virtue." Provoked, the plaintiff struck the defendant in the face with a kitchen towel. The defendant responded by hitting her eye (leaving the bruise that was visible for some two months), and by kicking her, causing some lameness. The North Dakota Supreme Court affirmed the plaintiff's recovery of $1,000 compensatory and $500 exemplary damages. The court rejected the defendant's predictable claim of self-defense, stating "a hand towel can scarcely be considered a dangerous weapon, and there is nothing to suggest that the defendant was a man of such timidity that the flourishing of a towel by a lady should fill him with alarm."

In 1961 the Supreme Court of Oklahoma entertained *Boston* v. *Muncy,* reversing and remanding an $11,000 jury award of compensatory damages for the plaintiff. The plaintiff and defendant had argued over the plaintiff's alleged promise to obtain an auto heater for the defendant. According to the defendant, the plaintiff took a swing at him, prompting the defendant to hit his assailant. The plaintiff's eye was put out by defendant's punch. The Oklahoma Supreme Court found the jury instruction on self-defense to be "reversible error." The instruction advised that the defendant could exercise the right of self-defense only if he believed himself to be in danger of great bodily harm. "This is not a correct statement of the law as applicable to the facts of this case . . . (Such an instruction) . . . is usually given . . . where a deadly weapon is used by defendant in his defense . . . Such an instruction, however, should not be given in an ordinary assault and battery case, especially where as here, it is conceded that the alleged assailant . . . *was using only his hand* and fist." (author's emphasis).

The Louisiana Appellate Court decided in *Mathew* v. *Stewart* that one "is not justified in using a dangerous weapon in self-defense, where the attacking party is not armed and when the person does not reasonably believe he was threatened with bodily harm."

Martial artists, of course, experience the same trials and tribulations as their non-trained counterparts. However, experts in the martial arts often are able to cope with confrontation and combat with greater calm and reflection than non-martial artists. Control of the mind and the conversion of fear into attack energy are goals of martial arts instruction. These skills have definite bearing on the performance of a karateka. The martial arts place a premium on *fudoshin,* the ability to remain calm in an emergency.

This presents several legal questions for martial artists. First, does the fudoshin enjoyed by the martial artist prevent him from claiming self-defense? Since there *can* be apprehension while calm, the martial artist likely can assert he acted only in self-defense.

Second, given the martial artist's superior fighting ability, both offensively and defensively, can there be "reasonable" fear of a battery succeeding? There certainly may be cases where the disparity in ability of the plaintiff to attack and the defendant martial artist to defend may be as great or greater than the disparity the North Dakota Court faced in *Power* v. *Meiers,*. The preferable view, it seems, would justify self-defense sufficient to prevent the attack. But reasonable apprehension nevertheless exists in the eyes of the law. A close analogy can be drawn to the example (Mr. A and Mr. B) finding the puny drunk liable in assault to the heavyweight boxing champion, even though the champ was in no actual danger of injury.

Third, what are the duties of a martial artist to warn his would-be attacker of the prospective victim's unique ability to frustrate such attacks? Muggings and barroom brawls are often averted by martial artists who warn of their powers. On the other hand, martial artists nervously chuckle when hearing the old joke about the karateka who, when approached by a robber, dropped to a low stance and barked out the warning "karate!" The robber retorted "crowbar!" and proceeded to separate his unconscious victim from his gold. The point is clear—warning may precipitate a more ruthless assault rather than avoid it.

Upon balancing the competing interest of the personal safety of expert martial artists with society's interest in stemming altercations, society's interests should prevail, and expert martial artists should declare not only their intention to defend themselves, but also their special ability to do so. Experts would presumably be able to defend themselves, even after warning, against most assaults short of one with a firearm. Here, and perhaps with other deadly weapons, no warning would be required since it would obviously jeopardize the capacity for self-defense. For like reasons, novices and near-novices in the martial arts should not be compelled to reveal more than their intention to defend themselves. Disclosing their training is not required by law—and should not be—since novices lack the expertise to make their defense deadly.

Finally, are martial artists justified in using the deadly force of their hands and feet in self-defense against non-deadly assaults? A *Boston* court held it was a reversible error to instruct a jury that bare hands could be used in self-defense only if great bodily harm was feared. That court considered hands to be non-deadly weapons, even though a defendant's punch put out the plaintiff's eye. However, the defendant in *Boston* (presumed not to be a martial artist) possessed no unusual capacity for violence with bare hands. The *Mathews* court, on the other hand, flatly declared that deadly force could not be used in self-defense against an unarmed attacker. When expert martial artists use their skills against unarmed assailants, it should be reviewed as the use of deadly force. The martial artist should be allowed opportunity to prove his defense was proportionate to the assault—that is, "deadly force" was controlled, and lethal techniques were avoided.

Whether you have a duty to retreat and attempt to avoid conflict prior to defending yourself turns on the degree or type of force utilized to repel the attack. In ordinary assault and battery cases, the defendant is under no obligation to retreat. He or she may stand their ground and "use force short of that likely to cause serious physical injury." This is allowed by law even if you know with absolute certainty that you can avoid threatened bodily harm by retreating.

The issue is not as well settled where you might refuse to retreat and use deadly force to defend against deadly force.

Courts are split as to whether a defendant must "retreat to the wall" before using deadly force. The majority of courts, centering largely in the South and West, hold dignity and sense of honor in esteem and permit the defendant to stand his or her ground and use deadly force against attacks which call for it. The defendant may even be privileged to kill his assailant.To use this deadly force, of course, you must believe that you are in danger of losing your life or will be seriously injured by your assailant.

While there is no duty to retreat when *non-deadly force* is used by one claiming the self-defense privilege, a duty to retreat exists where one uses or intends to use deadly force in self-defense. The restatement position (reported by John W. Wade):

> *The interest of society in the life and efficiency of its members and in the prevention of the serious breaches of the peace involved in bloody affrays require one attacked with a deadly weapon, except within his own dwelling place, to retreat before using force intended or likely to inflict death or serious bodily harm upon his assailant, unless he reasonably believes that there is any chance that retreat cannot be safely made.*

One expert refers to this as the view "preferred in a civilized community." It is followed by some 15 state jurisdictions. There are two exceptions. First, courts have continued the ancient rule that there is no obligation to retreat where the assaults takes place on the defendant's own premises. Second, the obligation to retreat is voided where the defendant can no longer retreat safely. If there is any reasonable doubt, you need not run. Clearly, no court would demand "detached reflection" in the presence of a drawn gun or an upraised knife. Some suggest that the proliferation of firearms all but reduces "safe retreat" to a moot issue. Retreat should be considered as just one element to be considered in judging reasonable conduct.

Persons trained in legitimate martial arts try to avoid street encounters as much as some people try to avoid taxes. Martial artists are instructed to always retreat if possible, and to stay and fight only if necessary for personal safety or the safety of another. The ethos of the martial arts (and peer pressure) forbids practitioners from flaunting their skills. Serious students are taught to "run with confidence" from confrontations. In fact, in many encounter situations, the best self-defense, even for a martial artist, is to simply run away.

Many martial artists impulsively retreat when possible. These retreating martial artists face no legal issues, whatever the jurisdiction.

The problem arises if a martial artist refuses to retreat when confronted with either deadly or non-deadly force. The assumption is that martial artists are capable of employing their hands and feet to inflict death or great bodily injury. However, martial artists are also capable of defending themselves through non-skilled methods (for example, grabbing the assailant and holding him or her until the danger passes). Also, martial artists can moderate the force of a kick or punch, vary a technique, or strike non-lethal areas on their assailant's body. And, of course, martial artists—like anyone else—can inflict deadly force by non-martial arts methods. Therefore, martial artists do not necessarily have to use their deadly skills in self-defense.

Refusing to Retreat

Here are four possible situations where a martial artist refuses to retreat and instead chooses to stand his or her ground and repel the assault:

1. *Martial artist uses deadly force against a deadly attack.* Here, deadly force refers to the use of naked hands and naked or shoed feet (not more orthodox deadly force, such as a knife or gun).

2. *Martial artist uses deadly force against a non-deadly attack.* For reasons discussed later, irrespective of the duty to retreat, the martial artist would be liable for excessive force, unless the court determined that circumstances justified the lethal response.

3. *Martial artist uses non-deadly force against a deadly attack.* Though this situation may seem unlikely, it is possible, and even sometimes probable, depending upon the expertise of the martial artist. A truly skilled martial artist is more likely to use non-lethal force successfully. Because of this, he is prone to try a non-lethal defense first.

The law covering the duty to retreat isn't specific when non-deadly force is used to repel a deadly attack. It doesn't seem fair, though, that the martial artist should be compelled to flee. He is using the same force allowed against a non-deadly attack, and so it seems reasonable he should be justified in disarming the assailant. Here, the martial artist does not always need to take full measure of his or her legal right to "match force with force" but rather undertakes to use a "lesser force" in his or her defense. Logically there should be no duty to retreat.

4. *Martial artist uses non-deadly force against a non-deadly attack.* If the court accepts that non-deadly force was used, in no jurisdiction would there be a duty to retreat imposed on the martial artist. But here is the hitch. Martial artists have reason to fear courts may perfunctorily categorize their defense as "deadly force," even where the facts belie this characterization. Though this will be discussed in greater detail, suffice it to say it would not be surprising to see many judges erroneously instruct the jury that the defendant is presumed to have used deadly force in self-defense, merely because the defendant is a "deadly" fighter.

Here, the trained fighter must examine his or her ability to measure the consequences of self-defense as well as to match force with (near) equal force.

Civil Law

To avoid liability for use of excessive force in self-defense, you may use only such force in repelling the attack as a "reasonable" person would have thought necessary under the circumstances. This has been characterized as "reasonable force." No greater force than is necessary to protect yourself is permissible. Another way of saying this, is that the force used in self-defense must be proportionate to the harm which you seek to avoid. For example, you are not privileged to use deadly force to prevent the infliction of a slight harm. A good illustration of this "proportionate force" doctrine is found in *Bannister* v. *Mitchell,* a case decided in 1920 by the Virginia Supreme Court. The defendant was brawling with the plaintiff's brother, a small one-legged man, when the plaintiff intervened by striking the defendant with her umbrella. The defendant's "self-defense" was to cut the female assailant with a pocket knife from cheek to ear. Affirming judgement of $650 damages for the women, the Virginia Supreme Court held that the force employed by the defendant was not proportionate. Moreover, "the use of his knife . . . under the circumstances was entirely unnecessary for his own protection."

There is one qualification: If you realize that someone attacking you with deadly force is incapable of achieving their purpose, you are *not* privileged to use deadly force in self-defense.

In determining whether the force used in self-defense is reasonable or excessive, American courts have looked to a number of factors. Some courts look to the amount of force exerted, the means employed to exert the force, the manner in which the force was applied, and the surrounding circumstances. Other courts have also looked to the parties themselves, considering such things as the relative age, size, and strength of the parties, their reputations for violence and who was the aggressor.

There is some difference of opinion regarding whether the defendant must intentionally or willfully exert excessive force before being subject to liability. Some authorities argue that only excessive force which is intentionally inflicted is covered by law. In *Dupre* v. *Maryland Management Company,* the plaintiff hotel guest harassed a bellhop who evidently had tried in vain to avoid encounters with him. Finally, the plaintiff assaulted the bellhop who promptly responded by fracturing his assailant's jaw. The trial court entertained the defendant's pleas of self-defense, but held for the plaintiff due to the "excessive force" used by the bellhop in his own defense. The Appellate Division Court, however, reversed the trial court's verdict, noting "one must know what he does will be excessive—an intent to inflict unnecessary injury must be established."

In contrast to *Dupre* stands *Nicholls* v. *Colwell,* a case decided by the Illinois Appellate Court in 1904. *Nicholls,* is not a simple self-defense case, but it has elements of self-defense law. The 40-year-old defendant, a former schoolteacher of the plaintiff, "playfully scuffled" with the young 18-year-old female plaintiff. There was conflicting evidence as to how willing a participant the plaintiff was in the "playful scuffle." In reversing the trial court's pre-emptory instructions for the defendant, the court remarked that if the defendant acted lawfully but nevertheless used greater force and violence than was justifiable under the circumstances, she "should be liable . . . whether the injuries were willfully inflicted or not."

The restatement explains in some detail the character of both permissive and excessive force in the self-defense setting. Courts allow that the defendant is privileged to use force in self-defense up to, but not in excess of, what the defendant correctly or reasonably believes necessary for his or her protection. Means of self-defense may become excessive where they do more harm than either the defendant intended or was privileged to inflict and this was reasonably foreseeable by the defendant.

Here are four examples of how a court would view the following incidents:

1. A man attempts to strike you with his fists. You are not privileged to knock him down if you can easily prevent him from striking you by holding his arm(s).
2. A man attempts to prevent you from leaving a room by standing in the only doorway. You are much larger than the other man and can readily push him out of the way. You are not privileged to knock him down.
3. A weak old man attempts to attack you with a knife. It is obvious to you than you can disarm the old man with perfect safety. You are not privileged to shoot him with a gun.
4. A man attempts to attack you. You size up the situation and can easily avoid his attack and disarm him. You are not privileged to confine that man in a room where you keep a ferocious watch dog.

In other words you cannot inflict (in self-defense) any greater damage than that which you reasonably believe is necessary for your own protection.

The restatement also discusses the legal consequences when the defendant uses force in excess of his self-defense privilege:

> *Force in Excess of Privilege. If the actor applies a force to or imposes a confinement upon another which is in excess of that which is privileged, (a) the actor is liable for only so much of the force or confinement as is excessive; (b) the other's liability for an invasion of any of the actor's interests of personality which the other may have caused is not af-*

fected; (c) the other has the normal privilege stated in this Topic to defend himself against the actor's use or attempted use of excessive force or confinement.

Comment *(a)* states that the defendant is liable only for force that was excessive; the defendant will not be liable "for so much of the force or confinement as he is privileged to apply or impose." However, comment *(b)* expands the analysis. Where there can be no neat division between privileged force and excessive force, the defendant is "held liable for all of the harm inflicted by the use of the excessive force." Two illustrations:

1. *Mr. A inflicts an offensive contact upon Mr. B, and threatens to continue it. Being stronger than A, B could easily prevent a continuance of the contact by seizing and holding A, and does so. B then unnecessarily strikes A in the face, breaking A's nose. B is not liable for holding A, but is subject to liability to A for the broken nose.*
2. *Mr. A inflicts an offensive contact upon Mr. B, and threatens to continue it. B could easily prevent the continuance of the contact by striking A a light blow. Instead he strikes a heavy blow, which breaks A's nose. B is subject to liability for the blow and the harm done.*

Turning from the restatement to case law, it is understood that one using excessive force to repel an attack not only loses the right to assert self-defense, but may also become liable in damages to the original aggressor. Three cases from Indiana, North Dakota, and federal district court in Louisiana are illustrative. In 1870 the Indiana Supreme Court decided *Adams* v. *Waggoner.* The plaintiff and defendant fought by mutual consent. The defendant became angry and stabbed the plaintiff three times. In affirming a verdict awarding the plaintiff damages, the Indiana Supreme Court held:

> *It is a settled doctrine of the law, that if one be attacked he may defend himself using no more force than may be necessary to repel the attack; but should he go beyond this, and use more than necessary, he becomes a trespasser himself, and his assailant, though first in the wrong, may maintain against him an action for damages.*

In 1972, a federal district court in Louisiana heard the case of *Baggett* v. *Richardson.* Two men boarded the plaintiff's ship, and the plaintiff began to struggle with one of the men. The man's partner joined in the scuffle and together the two men began to systematically beat the plaintiff for five to ten minutes with a pipe, resulting in multiple bruise and unconsciousness. The court awarded damages to the plaintiff because the defendants had used excessive violence in dealing with the plaintiff's original assault.

It is generally understood that the defendant may be privileged to use much greater force to protect himself or herself where the attack is by multiple assailants than when it is by a single assailant. The defendant becomes privileged by law to use force against a number of attackers that would be deemed excessive were there but one attacker. The justification for allowing defense by more forcible means when there are several assailants is that "a person assaulted by a mob . . . is necessarily . . . subject to greater terror and apprehension that when the assault is made by an individual . . ."

Martial artists practice fighting. It is the very nature of the beast that their capacity for *skilled* unarmed combat approaches perfection. Trained fighters can be "expected to possess a high degree of judgement" when confronted with fighting situations. With this training, and given a proper attitude, a martial artist "should be able to extricate himself from many situations without ever having to use excessive force."

Martial artists are trained to conform their self-defense to the seriousness of the attack. Gnats are not blasted with cannons. Neither are offensive, but reasonably harmless, drunks dealt with by deadly force. As one martial arts instructor stated:

> *You have to teach retaliation situations. If a person's just a drunk, you deal with him one way. If it's a group of hoodlums, you deal with them another way. And if it's a guy coming at you with a broken beer bottle, you deal with that another way.*

Trained fighters have a large capacity for unarmed deadly force. Those earlier "assault and battery" examples dealt primarily with the capacity of karateka and kung fu masters to inflict deadly force. The same is true of judoka. Neal Rosenberg, founder of Wisconsin judo, after an initial defeat, fought and beat a 450-pound trained fighting bear by pinning it to the mat for the count.

The martial arts are extremely effective against multiple assailants. Two more illustrations involving judoka illustrate the point. "In two similar incidents, Hiro Fujimoto (a judo expert) disarmed one knife-wielding assailant and broke the right hand of another tormenter." The *Dun's Review* article gave another classic example of judo's effectiveness against a gang attack:

> *At 46, Jerome Gillman, vice president of Richard Weiner Associates, a New York-based public relations firm, is not a violent man. But when "three big apes" jumped Gillman on a deserted Manhattan street late one night and demanded his wallet, the mild mannered 184-pound Gillman "instinctively did my homework . . ." He applied an elbow lock to the leader of the pack, neatly executed a classic* nage waza *and sent the startled mugger crashing to the sidewalk, rendering him "slightly unconscious." The other two punks fled in panic. They had made the mistake of accosting a business executive who happens to hold a second-degree black belt in judo.*

Several critical questions are posed for martial artists by the law of self-defense's reasonable versus excessive force issue. First, it is feared that an unspoken presumption may subject "deadly fighters" to liability for "excessive force" used in self-defense (due more to the characterization of the actor than the analysis of the particular facts and circumstances). What must be shown to jurists and legislators is the logical proposition that a capacity for deadly force does not indicate that the ability was used. This presents a problem of proof for the martial artists—and a problem of keeping inflammatory and legally irrelevant proof from the jury.

Martial artists have a wide-ranging arsenal at their disposal, from which they can spontaneously custom-make an appropriate defense. Not all self-defense should be presumed "excessive force" merely because it emanates from one with special skills to inflict excessive force. Instead of using deadly force, the martial artist can, for example:

— "Pull" his or her punches or kicks, as is done at non-contact karate tournaments in order to minimize impact.

— Strike or kick areas of the assailant's body which are not particularly sensitive or vulnerable, e.g., the side of the arm or right side of the chest as opposed to the groin or throat.
— Throw the attacker on his back gently instead of on his head forcefully.

If courts and legislatures accept the fact that martial artists can be selective in devising a defense, a different problem may be raised for the martial artist. When one has been injured by a martial artist claiming self-defense, courts may look to the seriousness of the injury, and assume that since the martial artist can select his or her defense, the nature of the injuries dictates whether the martial artist opted to use excessive force. Such a position would be unfortunate. While martial arts experts can ready-make a defense, they cannot totally control combat circumstances. Assailants have been known to run face first into the unexpected foot of a karateka. And while the aikido master may merely intend to subdue the attacker by arm lock until help arrives, he cannot prevent the aggressor from squirming—thus breaking his own arm.

Second, the factors listed by the restatement for courts to consider in determining if excessive force was used in self-defense seem well-suited to the special circumstances of martial artists. Several additional factors, however, could expand this list:
— What technique, if any, did the martial artist undertake to use and with what force?
— The physical characteristics of the martial artist compared with those of the other party.

The third issue deals with intent. In some cases it will not be relevant whether the martial artist intended excessive force. In others, this could become crucial. The danger is that courts may attribute this "intent to use excessive force" to martial artists due to their special training. This is as logically indefensible as attributing similar motives in "presumed excessive attacks." Much occurs in street combat beyond the control of even a trained and skilled fighter. Where this question of "intent to use excessive force" becomes an issue, courts should require the plaintiff to bear his burden of proof and no presumptions should be indulged.

The effect of these provisions is to significantly curtail the range of possible defenses open to a martial artist. The implicit assumption is that expert martial artists are trained fighters. They consciously and conscientiously train in various defenses to counter the myriad of possible attacks. For example, if an expert karateka were attacked, he or she could simply block punches and kicks until the assailant gave up the attack. If an expert jujitsu practitioner were attacked, he or she could lock a limb, without breaking it, until the assailant submitted or the authorities arrived. If an expert judoka were attacked, he or she could apply *shime-waza*, strangulation techniques, to the assailant until the assailant surrendered or painlessly lost consciousness. If an expert aikido student were attacked, he or she could repeatedly throw the assailant on their back until the assailant wearied. On the other hand, the karateka could block, then strike a killing blow to the temple; the jujitsu expert could break each and every one of the assailant's limbs; the judoka could continue the strangle after the assailant lost consciousness until the assailant died; the aikido expert could throw the assailant face first onto the sidewalk.

If the martial artist had a true choice between both alternatives, only the former, less forceful one would be privileged.

Also, there is reason to treat martial artists differently than non-martial artists when the actor is a victim of assault by multiple assailants. The law permits a non-trained fighter to use greater force in self-defense against gangs than against single attackers. the justification seems to be that the overpowering odds and greatly increased apprehension warrants the actor to use greater force in his or her defense. Martial artists, however, are not automatically granted privilege to use excessive force against multiple assailants. In their case, the odds are *not* overwhelming and the apprehension is *not* greatly increased. In fact, a martial artist is taught how to use the presence of multiple assailants to his or her advantage by "playing them off against one another" and defeating them one by one. For example, if attacked by three assailants, the expert martial artist typically would hurl one into another and quickly turn his attention to finish of the third. Of the remaining two, the martial artist would maneuver one in front of the other, incapacitate the assailant in front, then devote his attention to the third and final assailant.

This, of course, works better in theory than in practice. Nevertheless it often works as described. Thus, courts should look to the manner of defense and progressions of the combat to see if the martial artist is entitled to the privilege of using excessive force in his or her defense. In any event, no *automatic* privilege to use deadly force should be granted when the "victim" of a gang attack is a martial artist. If the "playing off" strategy succeeds, the martial artist should be no freer to use a deadly blow on a gang member than on a single assailant.

Finally, the "reasonable force" standard itself must be reevaluated when dealing with martial artists. Reasonable force is that force which a prudent man thinks necessary under the circumstances. When an expert martial artist is accused of excess force in self-defense, the standard should be higher, that of a "reasonable, prudent, expert martial artist." It is only fair that one with unique skills be held to a unique standard.

The force a person may use in self-defense is that force which seems necessary to fend off an attack and prevent injury. Easily stated, this sounds simple. In reality, this tit-for-tat force cannot be precisely gauged or measured. Generally speaking, the tool for measuring the force used in self-defense is "the yardstick of the reasonable, prudent man."

Hindsight, of course, remains 20/20. Hence, courts consider the circumstances at the time of the altercation and refuse to impose the burdens of "reasonableness" that looking back would demand. The defendant using self-defense is "not required to (have) nicely measure(d) or narrowly gauge(d) the force to the amount required from a deliberate retrospective view." Accordingly, at least if the defendant is facing a dangerous attack, he or she will not be held liable in damages for failing "to anticipate the precise effect of a blow with the fist."

Courts will take into account the "heat of conflict" and "impending peril" the defendant faces when repelling an attack. Typically, unless the force used in self-defense was "so excessive as clearly to be vindictive under the circumstances," the defendant will not be judged to have exceeded his privilege.

Martial artists are masters of measuring force. Karateka cleave melons placed on the bare stomachs of assistants by whipping samurai swords down within a fraction of an inch of the assistants' skin. Jujitsu experts apply only so much pressure to the limbs of their practice partners as necessary to execute the technique, yet avoid breaking bones. Judoka know with some intuitive precision the force needed to strangle a competitor into unconsciousness—not death. Aikido masters can throw opponents at varying velocities.

The simple explanation for this ability to measure force is the intense and constant practice of these techniques by martial artists. Measurement of force becomes second nature to these skilled fighters. Since it is essential for their practicing partner to avoid serious injury, martial artists must be able to "pull" their punches and kicks, "ease" their armlocks and chokes, and "soften" the impact their partners take when thrown to the mat. As to this last example, judoka continue to hold their partner, and pull up on their partner's body as he or she hits the mat after a throw (cushioning the fall).

Since martial artists are far more expert in measuring force than their unskilled counterparts, this special ability should be taken into account when determining whether "reasonable force" (i.e., that which seemed "reasonably necessary") was employed in self-defense. The martial artist should be held to the "reasonable, prudent expert martial artists" standard. A jury should have ability of martial artists to measure force described to them.

Recently a karate instructor was acquitted of the self-defense slaying of his father. The issue of excessive force was raised. The assailant's father, also a martial arts expert, attacked his son with a sword following an argument. The defendant fought a pitched battle with his father for 20-25 minutes, then tied *nunchaku* (wooden sticks held together with nylon) around his father's throat with the intent to cut off his air supply and subdue him. Instead of merely subduing his father, he inadvertently used too much force and killed him. This case, or its wrongful death counterpart, would be the type of case in which the martial artist's ability to measure force could become the dominant issue.

Criminal Law

As discussed earlier, a single event can give rise to both civil and criminal liability. Because of the importance of the topic, what follows will be an examination of criminal law as it addresses "measure of force in self-defense."

In determining whether the force used in self-defense was excessive, a key factor considered by courts is the physical disparity, if any, between the attacker the person asserting self-defense. This entails more than a simple comparison of heights, weights, ages, and body builds. Attention is paid to the relative ability of each party to harm the other. "An invalid with a loaded automatic in his hand can be more dangerous and cause much more terror than an unarmed, heavily muscled wrestler . . ."

Several courts have held that "disparity of parties" is conductive to findings of "excessive force," impairing the self-defense privilege. Five such cases give some flavor for the facts where physically superior defendants made self-defense pleas. In the aforementioned *Lyon* v. *Commonwealth* case, the court rejected the defendant's self-defense plea where the defendant beat up and kicked his 65-years-or-older, 135-pound, father-in-law for insulting him and shaking a fist in his face. Affirming the "large verdict" of a $500 fine and ten months imprisonment, the Kentucky Court of Appeals stressed that "it must be remembered that this was an aggravated case. Appellant Lyon was a young, able-bodied man while his father-in-law was an old, frail man who was as nothing in the hands of Lyon." The following year the Oklahoma Criminal Court of Appeals heard *Gober* v. *State.* In affirming the defendant's conviction for "assault and battery with force likely to cause death," the court held that the severe kicking and bruising inflicted upon the victim was unnecessary, since the defendant outweighed him by some 100 pounds "and, no doubt, would have easily handled him, were it necessary, without resort to extreme violence." The Tennessee Supreme Court addressed this same issue in its 1947 *Etter* v. *State* opinion. The victim had lost all his money to the defendant in a craps game. Angered, the victim thew a rock (it missed) at the defendant, then proceeded to strike at the defendant with his fists. Allegedly in self-defense, the defendant pulled a knife and killed the sore loser. In affirming the voluntary manslaughter conviction, the Tennessee Supreme Court stated:

> *In sports as well as fair play in human relations opponents are pitted against one another who ordinarily are propor-*

tionately matched. It is a well recognized principle of law that when one is beset with a single personal assault, not made by one of overpowering strength and force, the resistance thereto must be proportionate to the nature of the assault. In this case, the (defendant) was a much heavier man than the deceased . . . We can see no justification for the use of a knife.

Consistent with these opinions is *State* v. *McLeod*. Here, the participants' proportions were reversed, and the ruling reflected it. The defendant, a 63-year-old man with hands crippled by arthritis, squirted ammonia through his screen door at a 27-year-old ex-G.I. victim who had threatened him. Recognizing the defendant's right to self-defense the court emphasized the "physical disparity between the parties here." In *Jones* v. *Commonwealth* the Kentucky Court of Appeals ruled similarly. The defendant's wife had consulted with an attorney about divorcing the defendant. During consultation, the lawyer allegedly raped her. Enraged at hearing this, the defendant grabbed the attorney on the sidewalk outside his law office then beat and kicked him severely. Affirming the conviction for assault with intent to kill, the Kentucky court remarked in dicta:

Where there was great disparity in the ages of the parties or in their physical conditions, the older or weaker may be justified in using a deadly weapon to repel a violent attack by the other, although the assailant may be unarmed. But this consideration is available only for the purpose of preventing the defendant's otherwise perfect self-defense from being destroyed.

If the defendant uses "excessive force" in self-defense, he or she may thereby impair the self-defense privilege and become exposed to full criminal liability. This was the holding in *Lyon* v. *Commonwealth* (the defendant hit his old and weak father-in-law). The Kentucky Court of Appeals analyzed the legal consequences of excessive force in the following terms:

Appellant knew . . . (he) could easily defend himself against any assault which Scott (the son-in-law) might make on him. In other words, (he) was in no danger. In assault and battery, one may use such force only as is reasonable necessary to ward off the assault and to protect himself, but

> *he cannot, without incurring (criminal) liability, go beyond this and inflict upon his assailant any greater injury than is necessary to stop him.*

The Illinois Court of Appeals acted in accord with its 1971 *People* v. *Atkins* opinion. Following a minor automobile accident, the defendant and his victim stepped from their respective cars. As the victim started to reach in his pocket, the defendant knocked him to the ground then kicked him unconsciousness. Affirming the defendant's conviction for aggravated battery, the Illinois court remarked, even should it accept that the defendant acted in self-defense, his "conduct was far beyond that which was necessary to defend himself."

The most graphic case involving use of a deadly weapon (in the context of disparity of parties) is *Davis* v. *State*, decided by the Supreme Court of Indiana in 1898. The defendant, a 54-year-old, one-armed man, quarreled with the "victim," then voluntarily left the argument in hopes of avoiding a physical confrontation. A short time later, the victim—unarmed, but stout and robust—rushed at the defendant who responded by shooting a gun at him. Because the jury had been erroneously instructed on defendant's right to self-defense, the Indiana Supreme Court reversed the defendant's conviction of assault with intent to murder. As to these erroneous instructions, the court noted:

> *These instructions inform the jury that a person assaulted by another, who has no weapons in his hands . . . is not justified in using a deadly weapon in defense of his person. If that is the law, then in every conceivable case of a violent attack upon one by another, no matter what the circumstances may be, no matter what the disparity between the ages and physical strength of the two may be, the assaulted party must stand and take his chances of being knocked down and stamped into a jelly, or of being choked to death before he can lawfully use a weapon in his defense. . . . This is not the law.*

Some of these cases discuss "measure of force" and "excessive force" as though force employed to repel an attack could be precisely gauged. Courts facing the question, however, indicate that the defendant will not be held to some impossibly strict, neat measure, but will be allowed some attitude, given the "impending peril." As the Missouri Supreme Court stated in *State* v. *Hopkins*, "it is well settled that a person is not required to nicely gauge the amount of force necessary to repel an attack, but that he may act on appearances." The law will not require some "nice distinction as to the least amount of force necessary." "Measure of force" is a matter for a properly instructed judge and jury.

Because of extensive and rigorous practice, martial artists can be expected to possess a high degree of judgement when it comes to fight situations. If this training is coupled with a proper attitude, a martial artist should be able to extricate himself from many situations without ever having to use excessive force. Martial artists are instructed to adapt to the nature of the attack—that is, to vary self-defense postures and techniques to suit the danger encountered.

If the defendant reasonably knows he or she is about to be attacked, the defendant may resort to self-defense *before* being actually struck. The defendant "need not wait until the assault is made." As stated by the North Carolina Court of Appeals in *State* v. *Evans,* "the right to act in self-defense may arise from apparent danger." According to the Missouri Supreme Court's language in *State* v. *Daugherty,* the "right of attack, in some circumstances, may be essential to the right of self-defense." The *Daugherty* court discussed "anticipatory attack" thusly:

> *A person about to be attacked is not bound to wait until his adversary gets "the drop on him" or "draws bead on him," to use familiar, but significant expressions, before he takes steps to prevent these occurrences from taking place.*

A reasonable prerequisite for this right of "anticipatory attack" seems to be that the defendant be "without fault himself." It is equally clear that not all circumstances will allow the defendant to strike first.

One consequence of the training martial artists undergo is that they acquire a "sixth sense" about people, or as coined in Japanese—*genshin.* This "attack radar" warns expert martial artists of sudden attack. This is best illustrated by a favorite martial arts anecdote:

> *A master swordsman wanted to test his three best samurai disciples. He balanced a pillow over the door so that as each of them would enter one by one, the pillow would fall on*

them, like a surprise attack from an enemy. The first one stabbed the pillow on the floor. The second sliced it in mid-air. And the third one—who became the master's successor—did not enter the room, since he sensed the trick before it could happen.

Genshin has its roots in training and experience. Martial artists know and watch for the body language that precedes an attack. For example, this author's sensei instructed him never to watch the hands or feet of a prospective assailant; instead, martial artists should watch the assailant's eyes. A person's eyes markedly widen an instant before a blow is struck. The eyes telegraph the impending attack and the martial artist is taught to anticipate the attack, and if necessary, disarm the attacker before he strikes. It's been expressed as follows:

Is there really such a thing as a "sucker punch?" I tend to think not. If I am a martial artist in the true sense of the word, I'm going to be aware that something is about to happen, and I should be able to react to it.

The right to self-defense by anticipatory attack is allowed only when the defendant reasonably believes an attack is imminent. This is an area where martial artists should be judged by what other martial artists would find reasonable. This can be justified since martial artists not only will perceive an impending attack sooner than an untrained counterpart, but also since martial artists more likely will be accurate in the perception. Of course, this special standard might breed inconsistent verdicts. There could be circumstances where the anticipatory attack of a martial artist would be reasonable, and therefore privileged, and the anticipatory attack by a non-martial artist under identical circumstances would not be privileged. However, since martial artists by virtue of their training are better able than lay-persons to sense an attack, this inconsistency of result has a reasonable basis. The martial artist should not be penalized for keen sensory perception. Doing so puts a premium on late—perhaps fatally late—reaction time.

CHAPTER FOUR

The Effect of Consent

Chapter Four

Consent plays an important role in determining the liability for sports injuries. The general rule is that one can't recover damages caused by an act to which he consented. This also applies to persons who willingly prarticipate in sports or athletic contests. It's been explained as follows: A person who enters into a sport, game or contest may be taken to have consented to physical contacts consistent with the understood rules of the game. Consent in this context is often discussed in terms of "assumption of risk.'' The law has been summarized:

> *A voluntary participant in a lawful game or contest assumes the risks ordinarily incident thereto, and he is precluded from recovering from his opponent or other participants for injury or death resulting therefrom, since, under the maxim of* volenti non fit injuria, *one is not legally injured by an assault committed in a lawful game if he has consented to the game and the incident assault.*

This assumption of risk doctrine precludes recovery for injury or death resulting from participation in sports. Of course, these dangers must be *obvious* in order to be assumed. Assumption of risk, however, doesn't operate to automatically bar *all* recovery for *all* sports injuries. The doctrine is hedged with numerous qualifications. The sports participant assumes only those risks and dangers normally seen as within the scope of the sport in which he's participating. If intentional acts causing injuries go beyond ordinarily permissible behavior in the sport, there may be recovery for assault and battery. There also can be no assumption of the risk unless the participant knows the risks, and voluntarily consents to undertaking them. This consent covers only the particular acts to which the participant knows are likely to occur, or acts of a substantially similar nature. (A consent to a fistfight is *not* consent to having a finger bitten.) A sports participant doesn't assume the risk of injury resulting from negligence, although recovery may be barred under the doctrine of contributory negligence. Finally, although sports participants may assume the ordinary dangers of a violent game, they don't assume the risk of injury inflicted intentionally.

Boxing can be used to illustrate the consent of participants in a dangerous contact sport:

> *The consent is to the plaintiff's conduct, rather than to its consequences. If the plaintiff willingly engages in a boxing match, he does not of course consent to be killed, but he does consent to the defendant's striking at him, and hitting him if he can; and if death unexpectantly results, his consent to the act will defeat any action for the resulting invasion of his interests.*

This is qualified to the extent, according to some precedent, that the blow be struck with ''no greater force than is justifiable under the circumstances." Also, the person delivering the abuse must not be guilty of either recklessness or negligent conduct in striking the killing or crippling blow.

The restatement discusses the relationship of consent to sports injuries and legal liability:

Taking part in a game manifests a willingness to submit to such bodily contacts or restriction of liberty as are permitted by its rules or usages.

The restatement also defines the differences in the intent of rules:

Participating in such a game does not manifest consent to contacts which are prohibited by rules or usages of the game if such rules or usages are designed to protect the participants and not merely to secure the better playing of the game as a test of skill. This is true although the player knows that those with or against whom he is playing are habitual violators of such rules.

Illustration and examples describing the scope of consent in contact sports speckle the restatement. A few such illustrations and examples are reproduced here:

A, while tackling B, deliberately injures him. A is subject to liability to B, whether the tackle was or was not otherwise within the rules and usages of football.

A, a member of a football team, tackles B, a player on the opposing side. A's conduct is within the rules of the game. A is not liable to B.

A, a member of a football team, tackles B, an opposing player, while he, A, is offside. The tackle is made with no greater violence than would be permissible by the rules and usages of football were he "onside." A has not subjected B to a violence greater than, or different from, that permitted by the rules, although he is guilty of a breach of a rule. A is not liable to B.

A and B engage in a boxing match. A thereby consents to B's efforts to hit him, and to the blows which he receives in the course of the match and in accordance with its rules.

. . . There is no doubt that the consent would prevent recovery (where . . .) having confidence in his ability as an

artful dodger, A consents to let B try to hit him. B succeeds despite A's dodging.

Numerous courts have discussed legal liability for sports injuries. Two cases decided by state appellate courts in 1904 held that *accidents* occuring during friendly scuffling or wrestling matches don't provide grounds for legal recourse. *Nicholls* v. *Colwell,* the Illinois Appeals Court reversed the trial court's pre-emptory instructions for the defendant where the defendant allegedly injured the plaintiff, an 18-year-old female and former student of defendant's, during a "playful scuffle." In the course of its opinion, the Illinois Appeals Court quoted Hilliard:

An action for assault and battery does not lie where an injury is done by unavoidable accident in the course of a friendly wrestling match or other lawful athletic sport, if not dangerous.

A similar position was taken the same year in *Gibeline* v. *Smith* by the Missouri Appeals Court. The plaintiff and defendant were friends. The defendant saw the plaintiff each time he collected for a brewery at the saloon housing the plaintiff's lunch counter. The plaintiff and the defendant joked and scuffled frequently upon meeting. On the day the injury occured, the plaintiff was pushed into a showcase during their routine scuffle. The plaintiff and defendant then drank together and parted company, only for the plaintiff later to discover his ribs were broken from the impact with the showcase. The appeals court affirmed the verdict for the defendant, holding:

It is our opinion that if the parties to this controversy each voluntarily engaged in a friendly scuffle, and the defendant, without intending to do so, accidentally hurt the plaintiff, no action will lie.

To hold otherwise, reasoned the court, "would be to say that all untoward results from the play of men or boys in which they mutually engage would furnish a cause of action by the injured party." The court pointed to the "sanction which ages have given" to rough and dangerous athletic contests to support the view that scuffling of the type engaged in by plaintiff and defendant was not unlawful.

However, courts have held for liability in some instances where participation in a lawful sport gave rise to injury. As the

Kansas Supreme Court noted in its 1905 *McNeil* v. *Mullin* decision, ". . . an injury, even in sport, would be an assault if it went beyond what was admissible in sports of the sort, and was intentional." Accordingly, the Massachusetts Supreme Court in *Fitzgerald* v. *Cavin* affirmed a verdict for the plaintiff who had his testicles squeezed (a foul hold) by the defendant in what was supposed to be a "friendly wrestling match by mutual consent."

Sport and contest injuries occur frequently in the martial arts. These injuries occur both during regular class sessions and at tournaments. The two martial arts with the greatest sport flavor, organization and numbers of participants are judo and karate.

Judo has been described as "practically fool-proof against serious injury." Nevertheless, the sport is "made-to-order" for less serious but nevertheless painful and vexing injuries such as twisted elbows, sprained knees, bruised ankles, and swollen toes. Although broken legs and arms are rare, broken toes and dislocated shoulders are common. Some judoka have suffered double hernias and knee injuries requiring major surgery. Other judoka have had their head split open, requiring stitches.

These injuries are caused by the "lightning-fast throws and holds," joint locks, and strangles that make up the judo arsenal. These latter two categories of mayhem, joint locks and strangles, deserve particular mention. In a judo contest, one method of winning is to apply a joint lock to your opponent until he or she submits, the referee stops the match, or the bone breaks. Typically, the opponent knows when the technique has become inescapable and submission readily follows. A second method of defeating your contest opponent is to apply a choke or strangulation technique. The match is won when the opponent either submits or is strangled into unconsciousness. Chokes cut off the supply of oxygen to the brain.

Despite the sanctioned use of dangerous armlocks and chokes, judo contest injuries are reasonably rare. In the first place, all judoka are taught to slap or tap the mat, their opponent, or their own thigh to signal that they're being hurt. This command to cease is universally and quickly obeyed. Emphasis typically is placed on throws and pins since these safer techniques, not armlocks and chokes, account for most contest victories. (Judoka can also win contests with clean throws and solid pins.) Before judoka are thrown, they are taught the proper way to fall in order to avoid injury. As much as 90 percent of the body's impact with the ground can be neutralized by a correctly executed fall.

The net result of these surrender signals, discouraged use of armlocks and chokes, and meticulous training in how to fall, is to minimize serious judo injuries. Although not all injuries are reported, a variety of surveys taken at different times and different places have reported that *serious* judo injuries are rare. Colonel Oliver E. Wood, U.S. Military attache at Tokyo near the turn of the century, reported to the War Department that out of some 4,000 pupils who attended Dr. Kano's school of judo (Kodokan), not one was permanently injured. Dr. Koiwai, a physician and fifth-degree black belt in judo, contends that "no death attributed directly to choking has been reported since the development of judo in 1882." According to a Marine judo instructor, of the 50,000-70,000 marines who received Parris Island judo training over a four-year period, there was only one serious injury—a broken leg. A five-and-one-half-year survey conducted by the medical committee of the United States Judo Federation reported only 102 judo injuries. "Fractures (34) were most commonly encountered, followed by shoulder injuries (27) and dislocations (16)." Judo, it seems, results in less injury to judoka than karate to karateka.

Karate is an entirely different story. Like judo, it's common to see many ankle, knee, back, neck, and hand injuries, along with contusions, fractures, dislocations, and sprains. Additionally, one sees more serious injuries in karate than in judo. When James T. King, Jr., MD, performed emergency surgery on Betti Bell (a karate student struck by her sparring partner), he found that the karate blow had destroyed 60 percent of her liver. She was lucky to survive. Others have not.

Recently, a Flagstaff, Arizona, general surgeon saved the life of a young man whose transverse colon had been torn by a karate kick. An Atlanta ophthalmologist treated a patient who suffered a detached retina from the shock of a karate chop. Another physician recently reported to the *Medical Tribune* that a female patient had her pancreas severely damaged by a karate blow.

Countless other karateka have not survived the deadly blows received during karate instruction, training and competition. Several years ago, a young Californian died from kidney injuries the day following inept karate instruction. In the winter of 1974 a college student died after being struck in the spleen while practicing karate with a friend in Atlanta.

The occurrence of serious injuries and even death may be aggravated by the recent advent of contact karate tournaments. The Professional Karate Association has formed rules and procedures for full-contact karate competition. However, no single set of rules or procedures governs *all* karate tournaments. Some tournaments still require that punches and kicks be pulled to avoid dangerous injuries. Other tournaments permit contact, but require padding on the hands and feet and sometimes even require body armor. On the other extreme, still other karate tournaments permit full-contact and forbid use of any padding or armor. One such tournament advertised with claims of "blood and proof of honor, no holds barred, no protective equipment, and all descisions (sic) by submission or knockout." It is generally agreed that kicks and chops delivered at these "professional contact karate tournaments" can easily maim.

Research has discovered only one appellate case dealing with liability for a martial artist's sport's injury, *Klocek* v. *YMCA of Metro Milwaukee* decided by the Wisconsin Supreme Court in 1970. The plaintiff enrolled in a beginner's judo class offered by the YMCA. During the fifth week, the plaintiff was injured during a demonstration of *osotogari* (major outer reaping leg throw) by a substitute instructor, a first-degree black belt. The plaintiff charged the instructor with negligence, asserting that the substitute instructor was unqualified to teach judo.

In affirming the jury verdict for the defendant, the Wisconsin Supreme Court apparently considered three factors: the rank of the substitute instructor, the ability of the instructor to teach the technique which caused plaintiff's injuries, and the traditional negligence factors. As to the first factor, (the rank of the substitute instructor), the court looked to the internal rank requirements of Wisconsin judo and found the substitute instructor's first-degree black belt rank qualified him to teach judo. The court stated:

The substitute instructor was a first-degree black belt, a rank or status certifying to and requiring weekly school attendance, knowledge as to lower ranks, understanding of judo training and instructional methods, and qualifying as able to conduct classes with the approval of the ranking yudansha *or black belt instructor.*

The second factor was the ability of the substitute instructor to teach the technique which gave rise to plaintiff's injuries. Significantly, the court allowed expert testimony to establish the defendant's expertise. The highest ranking black belt instructor in Wisconsin testified that the substitute taught the osotogari throw as well as any instructor he knew. Apparently accepting the truth of this testimony, the court found for the defendant as to this second factor.

As to the third and final factor (the traditional questions of negligence), again the court affirmed the jury's exoneration of the defendant:

Reviewing the record, we find no reason to quarrel with either judge or jury. As the jury found, there was credible evidence supporting a no-negligence finding. As the judge commented, it is difficult to find any evidence that would support a different conclusion.

Liability for Sports Injuries

Two settings for martial arts sports injuries will be analyzed: those injuries inflicted by a partner or contest opponent and those caused by the negligence of the instructor.

When discussing contest injuries, a distinction should be drawn between judo and karate. Karate contest injuries occur more frequently and are usually more serious. Consequently, the standard for determining if *true* consent was given by the plaintiff should be higher for karateka than for judoka. The question is whether the karateka fully appreciated the risks related to competition. If not, grounds for legal action may exist.

A second consideration, particularly relevant to full-contact/no-padding karate matches, concerns exactly what the plaintiff consented to. Did the plaintiff consent only to a "contest" when he then engaged in a bloody battle? It runs contrary to some legal authority (and common sense) to allow the plaintiff to consent to negligent or intentional infliction of injury. Given the popularity and durability of boxing, there should be no legal problem with consenting to a full-contact karate match.

A third consideration is whether a rule violated by either contestant was designed to protect the player or to better the playing of the game. Consent is no bar to a cause of legal action if the purpose of the violated rule is to protect the player. It may be a bar if the rule's purpose is merely to better the playing of the game. A rule prohibiting judo throws off the mat defies exclusive categorization. Since the tournament sanction (the throw is awarded no points and the offender may be penalized) applies with equal force whether the victim of the bad technique lands on the border mat or in the bleachers. Also, a rule in some karate tournaments prohibiting throwing was put forth not only to minimize injuries, but also to encourage clean karate techniques and to discourage brawling. In fact, many contest rules at judo and karate tournaments serve dual purposes of protecting the contestants and encouraging the use of perfected techniques. The reasonable position seems to be that if the rule has as one of its purposes the protection of the martial artist, violation of such rule should allow legal action not barred by the injured party's initial consent.

A final consideration goes to the increasingly popular bare-knuckle, no-holds-barred karate bloodbaths. Any resemblance to the martial arts here seems wholly coincidental. The continued occurrence of serious injuries at such publicity-generating extravaganzas, with most awarding prize money to the winners (or survivors), may result in these vulgar displays being declared illegal (just as certain other types of spectator-geared combat has been declared illegal). Should this happen, contestants would not be engaged in a "lawful sport" and therefore in most jurisdictions would be allowed to recover for any injuries under the doctrine of "mutual combat." Consent will not prevent recovery.

Martial artists may also be injured due to the negligence of their instructor. The *Klocek* court provides the best available legal approach to determining if liability exists. Other courts, when faced with similar claims of negligence against martial arts instructors, should look to the three factors considered by the *Klocek* court. In addition to ordinary negligence issues, the Wisconsin Supreme Court looked to the instructor's rank and ability to teach the *particular technique* which was alleged to have been negligently taught or demonstrated. Expert testimony explained the significance of having attained the defendant's belt rank, and also expressed opinion as to the defendant's skill in performing the controversial technique. The impact of *Klocek* is that of establishing a "reasonable, prudent, expert martial artist" standard to experts in the Oriental fighting arts.

Mutual Combat

When fighters voluntarily and willingly square off, they're said to fight by "mutual combat." The majority of courts agree that consent to fight will not prevent recovery for injuries that might occur during the fight. The opinion has been expressed as follows:

> *It is generally held that consent will not avail as a defense in a case of mutual combat, as such fighting is unlawful. Consequently, neither party to a fight, in which both fighters voluntarily engage, may defend on the ground that the fight resulted from a challenge or an acceptance thereof. Each person injuried in a mutual combat may recover from the other all damages caused by the injuries received.*

This position originated with an early English case, *Mathews* v. *Ollerton.* That case was decided when trespass was still a criminal and not merely a civil offense, and thus the state had an interest in the case. The modern justification for allowing damages even though consent was given is from a two-fold doctrine. It stresses the interest of the state in preventing the altercation, and recognizes the deterring effect that permitting damages should have on potential fighters. There have been negative opinions expressed regarding this policy:

> *The cases (allowing damages after mutual combat) have been roundly criticized on the grounds that no one should be rewarded with damages for his own voluntary participation in a wrong, particularly where, as is usually the case, he himself commits a crime; that the state is fully able to protect itself by a criminal prosecution; and that the parties, if*

they give any thought to the law at all, which is quite improbable, are quite as likely to be encouraged by the hope that if they get hurt they can still win in court.

A minority of eight states, supported by the restatement, hold that consent to mutual combat defeats the civil action, except where the force employed during the conflict exceeds the consent. (Such as agreeing to a fistfight and having an opponent pull out a switchblade and stab you.) This assumes the fighters, when they consented, were aware of the usual risks in fighting. As noted in the restatement:

In the case of a fight or affray by mutual consent, each party gives consent to those blows from which he is unable to protect himself. But each consent to the other using such force as is reasonably necessary to defend himself against his opponent's attack.

Numerous courts have considered the problem of mutual combat. The minority or restatement position barring recovery is reflected in *McAdams* v. *Windham*, a case decided by the Alabama Supreme Court in 1928. While engaged in a friendly barefisted boxing match, the defendant hit his opponent in the heart, killing him. The plaintiff, the deceased man's widow, filed a wrongful death action. The Alabama Supreme Court described the fight both as "mutual combat" and as "a mere sporting contest." In either event, the court affirmed the verdict for the defendant, noting that harm suffered after consenting to combat creates no cause of legal action.

The position, which says consent to mutual combat *does not* defeat recovery for injuries received in said combat is well-supported. In *Lewis* v. *Fountain*, a 1915 North Carolina case, the plaintiff visited the defendant's home to stop the defendant from threatening the plaintiff's sister. The testimony didn't clearly establish which party was the initial aggressor. The North Carolina Supreme Court considered the matter of "first aggressor" critical and held "when two men fight together, thereby creating an affray, each is guilty of assault and battery upon the other, and each can maintain an action therefore." The 1884 Wisconsin Supreme Court case of *Shay* v. *Thompson* held similarly where two old farmers argued about the fence between their properties. The argument grew into a fight, during which the defendant gouged both eyes of the plaintiff. In affirming a $500 verdict for the plaintiff, the Wisconsin Supreme Court held "the fighting being unlawful, the consent of the plaintiff to fight is no bar to his action, and he is entitled to recover."

Apparently, the majority position allowing recovery of damages nevertheless does allow evidence of consent to fight to lessen the damages recovered. The Rhode Island Supreme Court in its 1923 *Teolis* v. *Moscatelli* opinion referred to this "mitigation of damages." The Maine Supreme Court in its 1892 *Grotton* v. *Glidden* decision preferred to describe allowing evidence of consenting to fight as a measure to keep down the amount of the punitive damages, but not to reduce the actual damages.

Martial artists are generally trained to shun street confrontations. The mutual combat which martial artists prefer is a professional effort to develop and perfect their skills. Called *randori* by judoka, or the free sparring of karate, this combat takes place only within the dojo or tournament hall.

Liability of the Martial Artist

A martial artist could be a mutual combatant in two settings: on the street and at tournaments (or in practice, but this is viewed with a different outlook and will be discussed later). Discussing tournaments first, it's likely that certain of them could be described as a series of "mutual combats." Some of the unrestrained full-contact matches have generated legal battles similar to hockey litigation. In fact, once judicial response has solidified in the hockey cases, there may be precedent developed which will help decide future karate cases.

If the description "mutual combat" applies to contact karate matches, the majority of courts would allow damages to injured participants. Courts aggreeing with the restatement position would bar recovery on the basis of consent, the same as if they viewed these matches as sports.

The second possibility for mutual combat is that of the streetfight. Two legal issues are raised. The first issue involves the duty to warn. The restatement requires only that the defendant warn of his intention to defend himself—and only if doing so won't hamper his defense. Nevertheless, as the previous analysis urged, the expert martial artist should also be required by law to disclose his particular ability to ward off attack. If this duty is imposed in a self-defense situation (and even if it isn't), it certainly should be part of the requirement to validify consent to mutual combat. In order for the opposing party to consent properly and legally, it's imperative for him to know how "un-mutual" the combat might become.

The second issue concerns invasion of the plaintiff's interest by an act of a different character. If the martial artist fails to disclose his special skills and a fight occurs, the opposing party never consented to the punishment likely to be received from a trained fighter. This is similar to consenting to a boxing match and discovering your opponent plans to load his gloves with buckshot. This being so, damages should be allowed under these mutual combat circumstances, even in a restatement jurisdiction. Identical analysis applies to the problem of "force exceeding consent."

Liability for Training Injuries

Consent to abuse cancels the liability of the act, and this will prevent any later recovery for injuries the person who consented might've suffered. The courts have taken a hard-nosed approach to cases involving battery, and have barred recovery where no public policy is violated:

> *The attitude of the courts has not, in general, been one of paternalism. Where no public interest is contravened, they have left the individual to work out his own destiny, and are not concerned with protecting him from his own folly in permitting others to do him harm.*

The consent must be to the *act*, not the resulting injury. The following example from the restatement illustrates the point. A allows B to punch him as hard as he can in the chest. Unknown to A or B, A has a bad heart, and dies from the blow. Because the consent was effective, there was no liability created and thus no grounds for wrongful death.

Harsh conditioning and disciplining are inherent in the legitimate martial arts. An uncompromising military regime of belt ranks and absolute unquestioned authority reign at the best martial arts dojo.

The style of conditioning is governed by the nature of the particular martial art. In judo, repeated series of 100 falls to the mat strengthen resistance to injury. In some forms of karate, conditioning is accomplished by sanchin breathing exercises. The student locks his stomach muscles while the instructor pounds away with fists, feet, and even bamboo poles. This serves to toughen the midsection and ready it for blows from an opponent.

Prompted by a different motivation, disciplining is delivered forms similar to conditioning, including the bamboo pole. In one reported appellate case, *Story* v. *Martin*, the defendant karate instructor maintained that striking the plaintiff after class was part of post-class disciplining. The defendant's witnesses testified that "a student of karate must expect rough treatment from his instructor, and that the instructor often physically disciplines the students during class." The defendant objected that the trial court did not allow enough evidence to which might prove karate instructors typically discipline students *after* class. Finding no evidence that the blow was related to karate instruction, the court upheld the verdict for the plaintiff. The important feature of *Story* is what the court did not do. Although it had the opportunity, the Louisiana Appeals Court did not condemn battery as it has occured in dojo disciplining.

Legal issues arise concerning both martial arts conditioning and martial arts disciplining. The legal questions regarding conditioning are well illustrated by examing sanchin breathing. Consent to be hit doesn't include consent to be kicked. If a martial artist prepares himself for a fist to the abdomen, and receives instead an unexpected foot, a cause of legal action may exist. On the other hand, this "surprise kick" may be part of the package to which the plaintiff implicity consented.

In regard to disciplining, *Story* gives attorneys for the defense some consolation, even though the instructor was held liable because the event took place during *post*-class disciplining. At least where youngsters are involved, martial arts instructors will now be given clearer guidelines as to their privilege to discipline.

Coerced consent to conditioning or disciplining does not bar recovery by the "consenting" plaintiff. Thus, an instructor could not rely on a student's consent if the student was bullied into granting it.

Future of Martial Arts

Until recently, the martial arts have successfully resisted the few attempts that've been made to impose outside regulation. However, efforts *are* under way to change this. Self-regulation may remain viable, at least in the area of training and competition in martial arts with strong central authorities. Judo stands the best chance of remaining self-regulated due to the effective leadership provided by the United States Judo Association (USJA) and United States Judo Federation (USJF). Also, judo is not known for the use of violent or offensive techniques, and the contest injuries that have blighted karate haven't plagued judo.

Presently, there are few if *any* legal restrictions uniquely imposed on martial artists. Apparently the restrictions on boxers and wrestlers are much more stringent than restrictions on martial artists. Any legislative attempt to regulate, license or register martial artists would face enforcement problems similar to those encountered by efforts at gun control. Black market and paperback instruction could prevent meaningful and even-handed enforcement of any limits on martial arts instruction.

Mandatory registration or licensure of martial artists is no solution. The capacity to employ deadly force shouldn't subject martial artists to any closer scrutiny than those who carry a pocketknife. Because martial artists are trained to avoid street encounters, pocketknife carriers, as a class, may pose a greater threat than martial artists.

Proposal for Training Regulation

Genuine martial artists and their con-man imitators have been free for many years to open schools with no greater state involvement than that required to obtain a business license. Of the 26 cities polled in a 1968 study, not even safety inspections are conducted at karate dojos. This seemingly careless government attitude has alarmed consumer groups and those fearful that martial arts studios may be converted into training grounds for muggers and unscrupulous toughs.

At least one state has responded. In Alabama, the state Attorney General's Office in conjunction with the state Consumer Protection Agency were prepared to propose legislation to regulate the martial arts in Alabama. These officers were concerned with the rip-off artists who offered substandard martial arts instruction to students trapped by confusing contracts. Karate leaders headed off these external regulations by forming the Alabama Martial Arts Association (AMAA), a non-profit organization to "regulate those persons who can teach the Martial Arts in Alabama, making them prove they are competent to carry their title." The regulation of martial artists by the AMAA parallels regulation of lawyers by the ABA and physicians by the AMA.

Other private associations like this should be organized. At this writing there exists no central authority to set standards for martial arts instruction. Creating a guiding authority is the second-best way to upgrade and standardize martial arts instruction. The best method would be direct legislative interference—something few martial artists want. These new authorities or associations could establish requirements for certification. The potential teacher would have to demonstrate competence in the martial arts he wants to teach. This is better than automatic certification for martial artists who possess high-ranking belts, since it's no secret that sometimes belts are self-awarded, or awarded undeservedly. (This is especially true when a flim-flam man creates a "new style" of karate.) Certification would permit an instructor to teach students only with approval of the guiding association. Public service advertising could warn consumers of the dangers—both physical and economic—of enrolling in martial arts classes conducted by uncertified instructors. A certification fee could finance any administrative expenses.

CHAPTER FIVE

Recommendations and Summary of Advice

his book has many suggestions for the courts and legislatures that someday will face questions similar to those contained herein. Some recommendations on how to deal with these complex issues are described in this chapter.

Martial Artist Liability Test (MALT)

This proposed test would be used by courts only where the martial artist is accused of assault and battery and cannot reasonably plead self-defense. The MALT test assumes: an assault and battery with the bare hands, feet (shoed or unshoed), or other animate part of an expert martial artist's body, when

used skillfully to inflict injury, is a malicious attack. This test contains the following elements:
— Was the martial artist an expert?
— Was the injury caused by a technique which the martial artist knew or should have known as a result of training?
— Was the expertise of the martial artist self-taught or "trained" by other experts?
— Was the injury caused by a martial arts technique as opposed to "streetfighting?"

Application of this test creates a presumption that the assault was malicious, entitling the plaintiff to recover punitive damages. The martial artist can rebut the presumption with competent evidence that no martial arts technique was employed to commit the battery. MALT brings the law in focus with the reality of fighting arts and the ability of their practitioners to inflict severe injury by use of bare hands and feet.

Standard of the Reasonable, Prudent, Expert Martial Artist

Many times the reasonableness of the martial artist's conduct should be measured by his or her peers, not by the yardstick of the reasonable, prudent (lay)man. This seems particularly appropriate in the following areas:

1. *Reasonable Force.* A person is only privileged to use reasonable force in self-defense. Given the martial artist's ability to measure force with some precision, and to choose from a variety of possible defenses, the martial artist should be held to a higher standard of reasonableness—that which appears reasonable to unskilled laymen. This should not be confused with MALT. No presumptions of excessive force are raised. Unlike the (aggressor) martial artist who batters another, the martial artist employing self-defense has the legal process forced upon him or her.

2. *Anticipatory Attack.* A skilled martial artist knows when an assault is imminent. Under the doctrine of anticipatory attack, the martial artist is privileged to strike first. Whether this belief was reasonable should be determined by what a reasonable, prudent, expert martial artist would have done in the same or similar circumstances. The skill, training, and reaction time of martial artists affect reasonableness to the anticipatory attack standard.

3. *Negligence.* Whether the martial artist's negligence caused the plaintiff's injuries raises a question of the martial artist's standard of care. The standard and its alleged infraction should be determined by looking to the martial artist's skill (when using the controversial technique) and belt rank. These considerations should go hand-in-hand with more traditional inquiries about negligence.

Duty To Warn

The restatement imposes a duty to warn if one intends to use self-defense, assuming such warning will not escalate the severity of the assailant's attack. This duty to warn applies to martial artists as well as others. However, an expert martial artist should also warn a potential attacker about his special ability. This should help deter the attack and it will not likely compromise the expert martial artist's self-defense. This expanded warning recognizes the camouflaged and greatly disproportionate ability of martial artists to injure an assailant.

Hands and Feet as Deadly or Dangerous Weapons

Hands, feet, and other parts of the martial artist's body, when used skillfully, can be "deadly" or "dangerous" weapons within the eyes of the law. These animate instrumentalities should be considered weapons, with attendant consequences, when *used* like weapons.

Focusing on *use* rather than adoption of a *per se* rule—i.e., "the hands and feet of martial artists *are* deadly/dangerous weapons"—avoids two problems. First, a *per se* rule ignores the fact that martial artists can abstain from using martial arts techniques or can, at least, abstain from using *deadly* techniques. Second, a *per se* rule leads to a quagmire of undesirable results when carried to logical extremes. Namely: How does one *disarm* the unarmed martial artist? What effect would the *confiscation* (of deadly weapons) statutes have? Would martial artists be guilty of *concealing* a deadly weapon by keeping their hands in their pockets? The more reasonable approach seems to be that the *use* of the hands, feet, etc., determines whether the "deadly/dangerous weapon" characterization is justified.

Shoe considerations lose importance in cases hinging on

whether the martial artist's feet were used as aggravated assault weapons. Since martial artists train in bare feet, often harden their bare feet, and many times can kick more effectively with bare feet, the judicial preoccupation with footwear should be a secondary.

State registration of martial artists provides no solutions. The enforcement problem would be staggering; an equal protection question would be raised; and no important state interest would be significantly served.

Presumed Malice

Malice or specific intent will be presumed from the circumstances. Some would argue that when the defendant is a martial artist, his special skill calls for a presumption that the injury inflicted was the injury actually intended. If the martial artist is the undisputed aggressor, this presumption might supported on public policy grounds. However, considerations shift when credible issues of self-defense exist. Unwittingly, the so-called "victim" may have exacerbated the injuries received from purely defensive techniques.

Martial artists should be allowed to rebut presumed malicious intent both with evidence of their personal reputations for peace and quietude; and with evidence that practitioners of their martial art are taught to use their skills only in self-defense.

Reasonableness Redefined to Reflect the Martial Artist's Special Training and Skill

Reasonableness underpins the privilege of self-defense. The issue is, "reasonable according to whom?" Due to their unique abilities, martial artists should be judged by a unique standard. This will not always work to the martial artist's benefit, but it is more fair and realistic than treating the martial artist like a layperson. This special standard would apply in the following four situations:

1. *Apprehension and Fudoshin.* The basic self-defense requirement is that the defendant be "apprehensive" of bodily harm. Martial artists are trained to display *fudoshin*, (calmness in an emergency) and this calmness could work to bar legitimate self-defense claims by martial artists. If peers are used to

measure the martial artist's "apprehension," a valid self-defense claim can be asserted.

2. *General Reasonableness of Conduct.* While this standard as applied to "apprehension" clearly works to martial artist's advantage, it just as clearly imposes a higher standard in terms of the overall reasonableness of the self-defense. Whether the martial artist can stop an assailant with less force than he actually used becomes important. Courts should be mindful of martial artists' special abilities, judging them by a "martial artist standard," and not sanction retribution guised as self-defense.

3. *Measurement of Force.* Defendants are entitled to use no more force in self-defense than is reasonably necessary. Unlike laypersons, martial artists can measure with some precision the force with which they apply their techniques. The only rational way to "test" this ability in the courtroom is by subjecting martial artists to the standard of their martial arts peers.

4. *Anticipatory Attack and Genshin.* Once the defendant reasonably knows an attack is imminent, he or she can "anticipatorily attack" in self-defense, inflicting the first blow. Enjoying a "radar attack system" cultivated by special training, the martial artist's *genshin* alerts him or her to the danger of attack. This is a prime example of the importance of the "reasonable according to whom?" question. While the martial artist's sudden anticipatory attack might appear unreasonable to a layperson, it probably would not to another martial artist. To avoid penalizing the martial artist for quick reaction time and a keen ability to perceive an imminent attack, martial artists should be judged by a standard of peers, not untrained counterparts.

Judicial Posture Toward Martial Artists

When confronted with a martial arts defendant, courts should determine his or her level of fighting competence before applying *any* presumptions or special standards. Experts should be distinguished from students or novices. Belt rank can be a useful, if sometimes misleading, rule of thumb. Black belts are clearly experts; brown belts may be. Professionally trained experts should be distinguished from self-taught or paperback-taught "experts." Novices, students, and the self-taught or paperback-taught martial artist usually possess insufficient proficiency to become the truly unique threat justifying unique treatment. Only the martial arts expert poses special problems for the criminal justice system.

Since criminal codes do not refer to any of the martial arts by name, no clear statutory guidelines exist to suggest the proper way for courts to deal with unarmed martial artists. Injustice will result if courts seize upon the defendant's status as a martial artist to support findings of "aggravated assault" or loss of the self-defense privilege due to "excessive force." Courts should examine facts. Relevant issues include: Is the defendant an expert martial artist? Did the defendant actually use a martial arts technique? If so, with what amount of force was the technique applied? Did the defendant deliberately strike or kick vulnerable areas on his adversary's body? To what extent did the acts of the injured party contribute to the injury incurred? Only when courts ask and find the answers to questions such as these will martial artists be treated justly.

CONCLUSION

This book assumes that current civil and criminal law lacks the legal theories and analysis to adequately cope with the issues posed by martial artists who can kill and maim without orthodox, inanimate weapons. Legal thought must expand, and lay to rest questions raised by the advent of the martial arts. As Justice Cardozo explained, "The inn that shelters for the night is not the journey's end. The law, like the traveler, must be ready for the morrow. It must have a principle of growth." The law must grow to devise standards governing the conduct and legal defenses of the expert martial artist.

Many of the questions in this book are raised for the first time. If these questions, and the answers given here, stimulate others to tackle the difficult issues generated when martial artists and the law interact, then the effort has been worthwhile.

APPENDIX

Some states have written statutes declaring certain martial weaponry "deadly weapons." The nunchaku and shuriken are commonly declared deadly, but history tells us the nunchaku was once an Okinawan farm implement. It wasn't until the farmers needed weapons to fight a Japanese occupying force that the nunchaku was pressed into service as a lethal weapon. Generally, the shuriken was used by fleeing warriors to scare or disarm an attacker, and was lethal only when dipped in poison (and in the movies). Many states now consider both strictly in a negative light. They ignore the fact that many martial artists practice with these weapons only as part of their art. Few are intent on using them "on the street."

However, even without special legislation, many weapons are declared "dangerous" or "deadly" by "case law," which is really "judge made law," and may reflect personal prejudices.

What follows (reprinted from KARATE ILLUSTRATED magazine) is a state-by-state examination of laws covering martial arts weaponry. As will be seen, the laws vary widely from one state to another:

ALABAMA

Brass knuckles, slingshots, or other weapon of a like kind or description. Anyone who carries concealed about his person brass knuckles, slingshots or other weapon of like kind or description shall, on conviction, be fined not less than $50.00 nor more than $500.00, and may also be imprisoned in the county jail or sentenced to hard labor for the county for not more than six months. *S13A-11-53.*

ALASKA

Explosive, incendiary or noxious gas; mine or *device that is designed, made, or adopted for the purpose of inflicting serious physical injury or death;* rocket . . .; bomb, grenade, (silencer) metal knuckles, switchblade or gravity knife, firearm . . .; rifle. *Sec. 11.61.200.*

ARIZONA

"Deadly weapon" means anything designed for lethal use. The term includes a firearm. *41-3151.*

ARKANSAS

Carrying certain weapons prohibited — Defenses — Penalty. — A person commits the offense of carrying a weapon if he possesses a handgun, knife, or club on or about his person, in a vehicle occupied by him, or otherwise readily available for use with a purpose to employ it as a weapon against a person. *41-3151.*

CALIFORNIA

Blackjacks, etc.; manufacture, sale or possession; concealed explosive or dagger; offense; punishment; exceptions

a) Any person in this state who manufactures or causes to be manufactured, imports into the state, or offers or exposes for sale, or who gives, lends, or possesses any cane gun or wallet gun, any firearm which is not immediately recognizable as a firearm, any ammunition which contains or consists of any flechette dart, any bullet containing or carrying an explosive agent, or any instrument or weapon of the kind commonly known as a blackjack, slungshot, billy, nunchaku, sandclub, sandbag, sawed-off shotgun, or metal knuckles, or who carries concealed upon his person any explosive substance, other than fixed ammunition or who carries concealed upon his person any dirk or dagger, is guilty of a felony, and upon conviction shall be punishable by imprisonment in the county jail not exceeding one year . . .

b) Subdivision (a) shall not apply to any of the following:

. . . (2) The possession of a nunchaku on the premises of a school which holds a regulatory or business license and teaches the arts of self-defense.

(3) The manufacturer of a nunchaku for sale to, or the sale of a nunchaku to, a school which holds regulatory or business license and teaches the art of self-defense.

. . . As used in this section, a "nunchaku" means an instrument consisting of two or more sticks, clubs, bars or rods to be used as handles, connected by a rope, cord, wire or chain, in . . . connection with practice . . . self-defense. *S12020*

COLORADO

Possessing a dangerous or illegal weapon—affirmative defense. (1) As used in this section, the term "dangerous weapon" means a firearm silencer, machine gun, short shotgun, or short rifle. (2) As used in this section, the term "illegal weapon" means a blackjack, gas gun, metallic knuckles, gravity knife, or switchblade knife. *Article 12. 18-12-102*

CONNECTICUT

. . . "deadly weapon" means any weapon from which a shot may be discharged, or a switchblade knife, gravity knife, billy, blackjack, bludgeon, or metal knuckles:

. . . "dangerous instrument" means any instrument, articles of substance which, under the circumstances in which it is used or attempted or threatened to be used, is capable of causing death or serious physical injury, and includes a "vehicle" as that term is defined in this section; *S53a-3.*

DELAWARE

. . . "Dangerous instrument" means any instrument, article, or substance which, under the circumstances in which it is used, attempted to be used, or threatened to be used, is readily capable of causing death or serious physical injury.

. . . "Deadly weapon" includes any weapon from which a shot may be discharged, a knife of any sort (other than an ordinary pocketknife carried in a closed position), switchblade knife, billy, blackjack, bludgeon, metal knuckles, slingshot, razor, bicycle chain or ice pick. *S222.*

FLORIDA

"Weapon" means any dirk, metallic knuckles, slung-shot, billie, tear gas gun, chemical weapon or device, or any other deadly weapon except a firearm or a common pocketknife. *S790.001.*

GEORGIA

(1) "Dangerous weapon" means any weapon commonly known as a "rocket launcher," "bazooka," or "recoilless rifle" which fires explosives or non-explosive rockets designed to injure or kill personnel or destroy heavy armor, or similar weapon used for such purpose . . . "mortar." . . . "hand grenade" or other similar weapon which is designed to explode and injure personnel or similar weapon used for such purpose. *16-11-121.*

HAWAII

Carrying deadly weapons; penalty. Any person not authorized by law, who carries concealed upon his person or within any vehicle used or occupied by him, or who is found armed with any dirk, dagger, blackjack, slug shot, billy, metal knuckles, pistol, or other deadly or dangerous weapons. *S134-51.*

IDAHO

Concealed and dangerous weapons — Possession and exhibition — Sale to minors. — . . . dirk, dirk knife, bowie knife, dagger, slingshot, pistol, revolver, gun, or any other deadly or dangerous weapon. *18-3302.*

ILLINOIS

Unlawful Use of Weapons. (a) A person commits the offense of unlawful use of weapons when he knowingly: (1) Sells, manufactures, purchases, possesses or carries any bludgeon, blackjack, slungshot, sandclub, sand-bag, metal knuckles or any knife, commonly referred to as a switchblade knife, which has a blade that opens automatically by hand pressure applied to a button, spring or other device in the handle of the knife; or (2) Carries or possesses with intent to use the same unlawfully against another, a dagger, dirk, billy, dangerous knife, razor, stiletto, broken bottle or other piece of glass, stun gun or taser or any other dangerous or deadly weapon or instrument of like character; or (3) Carries on or about his person, or in any vehicle, a tear gas gun projector or bomb or any object containing noxious liquid gas or substance other than an object containing a non-lethal noxious liquid gas or substance designed solely for personal defense carried by a person 18 years of age or older; or (4) Carries or possesses in any vehicle or concealed on or about his person except when on his land or in his own abode or fixed place of business any pistol, revolver, stun gun or taser or other firearm; or (5) Sets a spring gun; or (6) Possesses any device or attachment of any kind designed, used or intended for use in silencing the report of any firearm; or (7) Sells, manufactures, purchases, possesses or carries any weapon from which 8 or more shots or bullets may be discharged by a single function of the firing device, any shotgun having one or more barrels less than 18 inches in length, sometimes called a sawed-off shotgun, or any weapon made from a shotgun, whether by alteration, modification or otherwise if such weapon, as modified or altered, has an overall length of less than 26 inches, or a barrel length of less than 18 inches, or any bomb, bomb-shell, grenade, bottle or other container containing an explosive substance of over one-quarter ounce for like purposes, such as, but not limited to, black powder bombs and Molotov cocktails or artillery projectiles; or . . .

38 9 24-1

INDIANA

Exposing for sale prohibited — It is a class C infraction for a person to expose for sale any knucks, slung shot, or billy in any showcase or window along any streets or in any stores.

Chapter 9.35-23-10-1

IOWA

Deadly Weapon — Any firearm, knife, device or instrument designed to inflict death or serious bodily harm. *724.1*

KANSAS

Unlawful use of weapons. (1) Unlawful use of weapons is knowingly: (a) Selling, manufacturing, purchasing, possessing or carrying any bludgeon, sand-club, metal knuckles or any knife, commonly referred to as a switchblade, which has a blade that opens automatically by hand pressure applied to a button, spring or other device in the handle of the knife, or any knife having a blade that opens or falls or is ejected into position by the force of gravity or by an outward, downward, or centrifugal thrust or movement; (b) carrying concealed on one's person, or possessing with intent to use the same unlawfully against another, a dagger, dirk, billy, blackjack, slungshot, dangerous knife, straight-edged razor, stiletto or any other dangerous or deadly weapon or instrument of like character, except that an ordinary pocket knife with no blade more than four inches in length shall not be construed to be a dangerous or deadly weapon or instrument; (c) carrying on one's person or in any land, water or air vehicle, with intent to use the same unlawfully, a tear gas or smoke bomb or projector or any object containing a noxious liquid, gas or substance; (d) carrying any pistol, revolver or other firearm concealed on one's person except when on the person's land or in the person's abode or fixed place of business; (e) setting a spring gun; (f) possessing any device or attachment of any kind designed, used or intended for use in silencing the report of any firearm; (g) selling, manufacturing, purchasing, possessing or carrying a shotgun with a barrel less than 18 inches in length or any other firearm designed to discharge or capable of discharging automatically more than once by a single function of the trigger; or (h) possessing, manufacturing, causing to be manufactured, selling, offering for sale, lending, purchasing or giving away any cartridge which can be fired by a handgun and which has a plastic-coated bullet that has a core of less than 60% lead by weight. *Article 42. 21-4201.*

KENTUCKY

. . . (3) "Dangerous instrument" means any instrument, article, or substance which, under the circumstances in which it is used, attempted to be used, or threatened to be used, is readily capable of causing death or serious physical injury. (4) "Deadly weapon" means any weapon: (a) Any weapon from which a shot, readily capable of producing death or other serious physical injury, may be discharged; or (b) Any knife other than an ordinary pocket knife or hunting knife; or (c) Billy, nightstick, or club; or (d) Blackjack or slapjack; or (e) Nunchaku karate sticks; or (f) Shuriken or death star; or (g) Artificial knuckles made from metal, plastic or other similar hard material. *500.080.*

LOUISIANA

"Dangerous weapon" includes any gas, liquid or other substance or instrumentality, which, in the manner used, is calculated or likely to produce death or great bodily harm.

MAINE

A. "Use of a dangerous weapon" means the use of a firearm

or other weapon, device, instrument, material or substance, whether animate or inanimate, which, in the manner it is used or threatened to be used, is capable of producing death or serious bodily injury.

B. "Armed with a dangerous weapon" means in actual possession, regardless of whether the possession is visible or concealed . . . *17-a S 2.*

MARYLAND

". . . dirk knife, bowie knife, switchblade knife, sand-club, metal knuckles, razor, nunchaku, or any other dangerous or deadly weapon of any kind, whatsoever . . . *S36.*

MASSACHUSETTS

Penalty for Unlawfully Carrying Dangerous Weapons, Possessing Machine Gun, etc.

. . . (b) Whoever, except as provided by law, carries on his person or under his control in a vehicle, any stiletto, dagger, dirk knife, any knife having a double-edged blade or a switch knife, or any knife having an automatic spring released device by which the blade is released from the handle, having a blade of over one-and-a-half inches, or a slung shot, blackjack, metallic knuckles of any substance which could be put to the same use with the same or similar effect as metallic knuckles, nunchaku, zoobow, also known as clacker or kung fu sticks, or any similar weapon consisting of two sticks of wood, plastic or metal connected at one end by a length of rope, chain, wire or leather, a shuriken or any similar pointed starlike object intended to injure a person when thrown, or a manrikigusari or similar length of chain having weighted ends; or whoever, when arrested upon a warrant for an alleged crime, or when arrested while committing a breach of disturbance of the public peace, is armed with or has on his person or, has on his person or under his control in a vehicle, a billy or other dangerous weapon other than those herein mentioned, and those mentioned in Paragraph (a) shall be punished by imprisonment for not less than two-and-one-half years nor more than five years in the state prison, or for not less than six months nor more than two-and-one-half years in a jail or a house of correction, except that, if the court finds that the defendant has not been previously convicted of a felony, he may be punished by a fine of not more than fifty dollars or by imprisonment for not more than two-and-one-half years in a jail or house of correction. *S10.*

MICHIGAN

Any person who shall manufacture, sell, offer for sale or possess any machine gun or firearm which shoots or is designed to shoot automatically more than 1 shot without manual reloading, by a single function of the trigger, or any muffler, silencer or device for deadening or muffling the sound of a discharged firearm, or any bomb, or bomb shell, blackjack, slung shot, billy, metallic knuckles, sand-club, sand bag, or bludgeon or any gas ejecting device, weapon, cartridge, container or contrivance designed or equipped for or capable of ejecting any gas which will either temporarily or permanently disable, incapacitate, injure or harm any person with whom it comes in contact, shall be guilty of a felony, punishable by imprisonment in the state prison for not more than 5 years or by a fine of not more than $2,500.00. *750.224*

Carrying Firearms or Dangerous Weapon with Unlawful Intent — Any person who, with intent to use the same unlawfully against the person of another, goes armed with a pistol or other firearm or dagger, dirk, razor, stiletto, or knife having a blade over 3 inches in length, or any other dangerous or deadly weapon or instrument, shall be guilty of a felony, punishable by imprisonment in the state prison for not more than 5 years or by a fine of not more than $2,500. *750.226*

MINNESOTA

Minnesota does not define "dangerous" or "deadly" weapons.

MISSISSIPPI

Deadly weapons — carrying deadly weapon and use of imitation firearm prohibited — penalties. Any person who carries, concealed in whole or in part, any bowie knife, dirk knife, butcher knife, switchblade knife, metallic knuckles, blackjack, sling shot, pistol, revolver, or any rifle with a barrel of less than sixteen (16) inches in length, or any shotgun with a barrel of less than eighteen (18) inches in length, machine gun or any fully automatic firearm or deadly weapon, or any muffler or silencer for any firearm, whether or not it is accompanied by a firearm . . . *S97-37-1.*

MISSOURI

. . . "Dangerous instrument" means any instrument, article or substance, which, under the circumstances in which it is used, is readily capable of causing death or other serious physical injury. (9) "Deadly Weapon" means any firearm, loaded or unloaded, or any weapon from which a shot, readily capable of producing death or serious physical injury may be discharged, or a switchblade knife, dagger, billy, blackjack or metal knuckles. *556.061.*

MONTANA

Weapon means any instrument, article, or substance which

regardless of its primary function is readily capable of being used to produce death or serious bodily harm. *45-2-101 (71).*

NEBRASKA

Nebraska does not define "dangerous" or "deadly" weapons.

NEVADA

. . . (a) Manufacture or cause to be manufactured, or import into the state, or keep, offer or expose for sale, or give, lend or possess any instrument or weapon of any kind commonly known as a switchblade knife, blackjack, slung shot, billy, sand-club, sandbag or metal knuckles; or

(b) Carry concealed upon his person: (1) Any explosive substance, other than fixed ammunition; (2) Any dirk, dagger or dangerous knife; or (3) Any pistol, revolver or other firearm, or other dangerous or deadly weapon. *202.350*

NEW HAMPSHIRE

"Deadly weapon" means any firearm, knife or other substance or thing which, in the manner it is used, intended to be used, or threatened to be used, is known to be capable of producing death or serious bodily injury. *625:11.*

NEW JERSEY

Any dangerous instrument of the kinds known as a blackjack, slung shot, billy, sand-club, sandbag, bludgeon, metal knuckles, cestus or similar leather band studded with metal for fitting on the knuckles, loose wood impregnated with metal filings, or razor blades imbedded in wood slivers, dagger, dirk, dangerous knife or knife as defined . . . stiletto, grenade, bomb or other explosive, other than fixed ammunition, except as such person may be licensed to carry.

2A:151-41.

NEW MEXICO

New Mexico does not define "dangerous" or "deadly" weapons.

NEW YORK

"Deadly weapon" means any loaded weapon from which a shot, readily capable of producing death or other serious physical injury, may be discharged, or a switchblade knife, gravity knife, dagger, billy, blackjack, or metal knuckles. "Dangerous instrument" means any instrument, article or substance, including a "vehicle" as that term is defined in this section, which, under the circumstances in which it is used, attempted to be used or threatened to be used, is readily capable of causing death or other serious physical injury.

S10.00

NORTH CAROLINA

If anyone, except when on his own premises, shall willfully and intentionally carry concealed about his person any bowie knife, dirk, dagger, sling shot, loaded cane, brass, iron or metallic knuckles, razor, pistol, gun or other deadly weapon of like kind, he shall be guilty of a misdemeanor punishable by a fine not to exceed five hundred dollars ($500.00), imprisonment for not more than six months, or both. *S14-269.*

NORTH DAKOTA

1. Any instrument or weapon of the kind usually known as a blackjack, slung shot, billy, sand-club, sand bag, bludgeon, metal knuckles, knife with a blade of five inches (12.7 centimeters) or more, switchblade knife of any length, or any sharp or dangerous weapon which may be employed in the attack or defense of a person. 2. Any gun or dangerous firearm whether the same is loaded or unloaded. *62-03-01.*

OHIO

"Deadly weapon" means any instrument, device, or thing capable of inflicting death, and designed, or specially adapted for use as a weapon, or possessed, carried, or used as a weapon. *2923.11.*

OKLAHOMA

Oklahoma laws fail to define "deadly" or "dangerous" weapons.

OREGON

Except as provided . . . any person who manufactures, causes to be manufactured, sells, keeps for sale, offers, gives, loans, carries or possesses an instrument or weapon having a blade which projects or swings into position by force of a spring or other device and commonly known as a switchblade knife or an instrument or weapon commonly known as a blackjack, slung shot, billy, sand-club, sandbag, sap glove or metal knuckles, or who carries a dirk, dagger or stiletto commits a Class A misdemeanor. *166.510*

PENNSYLVANIA

"Deadly weapon." Any firearm, whether loaded or unloaded or any device designed as a weapon and capable of producing death or serious bodily injury, or any other device or instrumentality which, in the manner in which it is used or intended to be used is calculated or likely to produce death or serious bodily injury. *S2301.*

RHODE ISLAND

Weapons other than firearms prohibited. — No person shall carry or possess or attempt to use against another, any instrument or weapon of the kind commonly known as a blackjack, sling shot, billy, sand-club, sandbag, metal knuckles, bludgeon, or the so-called "Kung-Fu" weapons, nor shall any person, with intent to use the same unlawfully against another, carry or possess a dagger, dirk, stiletto, sword-in-cane, bowie knife, or other similar weapon designed to cut and stab another, nor shall any person wear or carry concealed upon his person, any of the aforesaid instruments or weapons, or any razor, or knife of any description having a blade of more than three (3) inches in length . . . *11-47-42.*

SOUTH CAROLINA

South Carolina does not define "dangerous" or "deadly" weapons.

SOUTH DAKOTA

Dangerous or Deadly Weapons — Any firearm, knife or device, instrument, material or substance whether animate or inanimate which is calculated or designed to inflict death or serious bodily harm or by the manner in which it is used is likely to inflict deadly or serious bodily harm. *221.2.*

TENNESSEE

. . . such as bowie knife, black jack, knuckles, slung shot, pistols, burglar's tools, or any other weapon or device which is denominated as unlawful under the statutes . . . *39-6-1707*

TEXAS

"Deadly weapon" means (A) a firearm or anything manifestly designed, made, or adapted for the purpose of inflicting death or serious bodily injury; or (B) anything that in the manner of its use or intended use is capable of causing death or serious bodily injury. *S1.07.*

UTAH

"Dangerous weapon" means any item that in the manner of its use or intented use is capable of causing death or serious bodily injury. In construing whether an item, object, or thing not commonly known as a dangerous weapon is a dangerous weapon, the character of the instrument, object, or thing; the character of the injury produced, if any; and the manner in which the instrument, object, or thing was used shall be determinative. *76-10-501.*

VERMONT

Slung shot, blackjack, brass knuckles—Use or possession. A person who uses a slung shot, blackjack, brass knuckles or similar weapon against another person, or attempts to do, or who possesses a slung shot, blackjack, brass knuckles, or similar weapon, with intent so to use it, shall be imprisoned . . . *S4001.*

VIRGINIA

If any person carry about his person, hid from common observation, any pistol, revolver, or other weapon designed or intended to propel a missile of any kind; dirk, bowie knife, switchblade knife, razor, slingshot, metal knucks, blackjack, any flailing instrument consisting of two or more rigid parts connected in such a manner as to allow them to swing freely, which may be known as a nunchahka, nunchuck, nunchaku, shuriken, or fighting chain, or any weapon of like kind, he shall be guilty of a Class 1 misdemeanor, and such weapon shall be forfeited to the Commonwealth and may be seized by an officer as forfeited. *S18.2-308.*

WASHINGTON

. . . who shall manufacture, sell or dispose of or have in his possession any instrument or weapon of the kind usually known as slung shot, sand-club, or metal knuckles, or spring blade knife or any knife the blade of which is automatically released by a spring mechanism or other mechanical device, or any knife having a blade which opens, or falls, or is ejected into position by the force of gravity, or by an outward, downward, or centrifugal thrust or movement; who shall furtively carry with intent to conceal any dagger, dirk, pistol, or other dangerous weapon; or who shall use any contrivance or device for suppressing the noise of a firearm, shall be guilty of a gross misdemeanor. *9.41.250.*

WEST VIRGINIA

. . . carry about his person any revolver or pistol, dirk, bowie knife, slung shot, razor, billy, metallic or other false knuckles, or other dangerous or deadly weapon of like kind or character, he shall be guilty of a misdemeanor, and, upon conviction thereof shall be imprisoned . . . *S61-7-1.*

WISCONSIN

"Dangerous weapon" means any firearm, whether loaded or unloaded, or any device designed as a weapon and capable of producing death or great bodily harm, or any other device or instrumentality which, in the manner it is used or intended to be used, is calculated or likely to produce death or great bodily harm. . . . *any electric weapon, as defined in s.941. 295(4) . . .* 939.22

WYOMING

"Deadly weapon" means but is not limited to firearms or incendiary material, motorized vehicle, an animal or instrument, material or substance, which in the . . . may be intended to be used is reasonably capable of producing . . . bodily injury; *S6-1-104.*